Time _and_ Poetry

by Jay Bryant

DORRANCE
PUBLISHING CO
EST. 1920
PITTSBURGH, PENNSYLVANIA 15238

Dorrance Publishing Co
585 Alpha Drive
Suite 103
Pittsburgh, PA 15238
Visit our website at www.dorrancebookstore.com

ISBN: 979-8-89211-303-8
eISBN: 979-8-89211-801-9

ACKNOWLEDGEMENTS

I wish to extend my appreciation to the following deserving persons, as well as others, whose names I have regrettably forgotten, or whose contributions I have shamefully failed to sufficiently recognize:

My mother, Vi Bryant, who occasionally used to enliven the day when, for no apparent reason, she would suddenly cry out, "Hail to thee, blithe spirit/Bird thou never wert/That from heaven, or near it/Pourest thy full heart/In profuse strains/Of unpremeditated art." And for acquiring, I know not how, that incredible bookcase filled with a cheap matched set of about a hundred of the great classics of literature, from Homer to Hemingway, which from my earliest memory challenged me to read. And my father, Al Bryant, too, who sent home a letter from the war telling her he was sending a book of poetry, which turned out to be *The Complete Works of Robert Service*. I read "Lipstick Liz" during oral presentations one sixth-grade morning, for which I was sternly, though privately, chastised by Mrs. Davis.

My late wife of fifty-four years, Susan Bohlen Bryant, who on our first date, told me she hated poetry, but who was responsible for ordering me to write the second Christmas poem, as well as numbers 3–20. And for many other things, too, including being the love of my life.

Our daughters, Amy Weaver and Amanda Mason, whose support I can never repay, and who may yet get to pick out my nursing home, as they have so often promised and/or threatened.

My brother Jon, my niece Hannah, and my granddaughter Madelyn, who allowed me to read an original poem at their weddings. And Syd Rothrock, who did me the same honor at his mother's funeral. Though it would be inappropriate to include such personal verses in this collection, I regard them as important creative efforts nonetheless.

Eric Nisula and Gene Owen, friends of my youth, who read and encouraged various early attempts.

Ruth Goddard and Kaaren Erickson, girlfriends of my youth, each of whom has a poem herein, and Joyce Nadeau, first of all of them, who I sort of picked out of a lineup, and who has no poem but did leave a memory worthy of one upon a dark midnight when she ran, barefoot in faux leopard shortie pajamas, across her front lawn and leapt into the back seat of Jimmy Rasmussen's car with fervent hugs and kisses for me. She had been unable to go to the movies that night and had arranged for me to take her next door neighbor, Delores, instead. When we pulled up to the side of the road between their houses, Delores bolted from the car like a scared rabbit and left the rear door wide open for any leopards that might be lurking in the neighborhood.

Miss Ham in Harmony, Mr. Smith in Simsbury and, in Evanston, Professors Nethercott, Bacon, Hungerford, and Maloney (as well as the great Stephen Spender, who lectured there one year), teachers who extended my understanding and appreciation of literature.

John Weicher, the best friend I have ever had and for whom my respect knows no bounds. B. and Susan Oglesby, likewise. And the estimable Sheila Whalen, although our joint literary fantasies never came true.

Certified ghostwriter Donna Mosher, once my student, who has been kind enough to read so much of what I have written, and brave enough to tell me when it was garbage.

Brian Sweeney, who will be disappointed that "George Dunne, What Have You Done," a TV commercial in verse that startled Chicago voters one fall, did not make the cut, as I decided not to include any political screeds. And Colonel Glenn Lackey and his best wife, the wonderful Claudia, who startled *me* three decades later when she revealed she had been married to Dunne at the time. *Awk*ward.

Wilma Goldstein, my favorite Jewish American Princess, who will be disappointed that "Princesses primp and princesses preen/Screw the Ingénues, God Save the Queen," her private epigram, did not make it. Oh, wait a minute. I guess it did after all.

IV

A great many North Carolinians who made Susan and me welcome when we "came to Dixie," especially Jack and Grace Hawke, John Turner, Claude Pope and Jeff Morse.

Molly Mead, who challenges me.

My cousin Marilyn LaGrow, who helped make "Archipelago" possible, and for much else.

My brother-in-law, benefactor, and co-author of our two books, Greg Bohlen.

Ricardo Maldonado, Mary Sutton, and Michelle Campagna of the Academy of American Poets, who graciously and expertly facilitated my research for *Time and Poetry*.

The staff and consultants at Dorrance Publishing, including Ben Altomari, Annabelle Harsch, Kaitlyn Ciancio, Wylie Stephenson and especially my editor and coach, Rachael Bindas.

And certainly Kay Laney, my dear friend since we were four-year-olds, who comforts me to this day.

And anyone else who, reading this list, wonders why they were not included. No doubt you should have been.

FOREWORD

This collection of my work in poetry and prose spans sixty years, the first poem having been written in 1963 and the latest in 2023. Some are romantic, some are angry, one is, I hope you will agree, hilarious, while another is sloppily sentimental ("Amy in a Light Green Blanket"). A few have a Christmas theme and were written as Christmas cards in the years indicated. In all, I wrote twenty Christmas poems, one a year between 1966 and 1985. My wife made me do it. Thank you, Susan. As usual, you were right. (See "A Christmas to Remember" for the full story of how the series began.)

My very first attempt at writing a serious poem came in the summer after I graduated high school. The original version read:

> *Mightily upward the spring tree thrusts*
> *Its skeleton bared for all to see*
> *Deep in the earth, its fare to seek*
> *The incipient life-root digs*
> *While the leaf-buds crawl like ladybugs*
> *Around the still-dead twigs.*

I called it "Elm in Early April." It didn't take me long to realize it wasn't very good, and I moved on to other things. As I prepared this collection, I remembered it, and asked myself *why* it wasn't very good. Not nearly good enough to be included herein. In looking at it for the first time in decades, I saw it was built on two genuinely good images: a bare-limbed tree as a skeleton, which was hardly original, and the buds as ladybugs, which was. That encouraged me to keep examining it.

I realized immediately that the title was wrong. When you say the word "elm" to someone, their mind immediately conjures a large, mature tree, like the one that shaded the front lawn at our Wake Forest house. But that was not the image I had in mind when I wrote the poem. I was thinking of a yearling

1

tree, a sapling, in the spring of its life as well as the spring of the year. So I changed the title to "Sapling in Early April."

Somewhere about that point, I committed myself to rewriting the poem. To be sure, it was never going to be more than a simple lyric still life, but with the two good images, it had potential to be a nice little verse. I decided to change the first word, "mightily," to "bravely," a better choice for a sapling, which is anything but mighty. But it *is* brave, challenging the new world to which it has awakened after its very first hibernation. I decided the phrase "spring tree" was clumsy and put "sapling" in there instead, knowing it would mean I would have to change the title again.

I also understood that it needed another two lines and division into two stanzas. I thought about how the clouds of April are often close to the ground, fog, really. I wanted the clouds to *caress* the tree, and I thought immediately of waves caressing the sea, so I wrote,

> *While the frothy clouds caress the tree*
> *As the waves caress the sea.*

which gave me a rhyme. But I realized "the tree" was weak, and I didn't really need the rhyme, so after some thought, I chose "its limbs" instead, which also strengthened the erotic sense implied by the use of "caress" which I liked. But that meant "frothy" was wrong: it was either too erotic, almost pornographic, suggesting semen, or not the least bit erotic. So I changed it to "gentle," making the line read "While the gentle clouds caress its limbs." In the next line, I debated the first "the" and decided it was superfluous.

Then I thought, if the clouds are really fog, why not call them fog? It would have to be fogs, plural, though, because otherwise I would throw the scansion off with "caresses," instead of "caress." So it was "fogs caress." I liked that. But what about the "gentle"? It was okay, but could it be better? April fogs are warm. You feel it when you step out in the morning. The March chill is gone, and the temperature has become mild. I decided that the right word was "warming." So the line now read, "While the warming fogs caress its limbs." Yes.

The hint of eroticism is preserved and the coming of spring is affirmed. But the change from clouds to fogs weakens the comparison with the ocean waves. The waves/ocean line also has a more important problem in that it takes the reader away from the scene. Is there another way to end the stanza? I thought about what the limb's response to the caresses would be and was rewarded by the word "shudder." So I wrote, "And they shudder gratefully." Gratefully. Yes, I liked that.

I turned to the second stanza, which at this point read: "Deep in the earth, its fare to seek/The incipient life-root digs/While the leaf-buds crawl like ladybugs/Around the still-dead twigs." Incipient? No. The root is not incipient. It's been there all along, working to feed the tree even in the winter. It never stops working, never stops eating the underground microbes on which it feeds. It is *insatiable*. Eureka! One final word still grated, the made-up compound "still-dead." The twigs were not still dead. They were...wakening. No, *awakening*. The ladybugs were crawling around, no, *along* the *awakening* twigs.

I still had the title to deal with. Way back when, I had chosen to make my tree an elm, mainly because the words "elm in early..." constituted not only an alliteration, but also a use of the poetic device called augmentation, although I wouldn't have known that word until a couple of years after I wrote the original and had taken some poetry courses at Northwestern. Now I remembered Professor Bacon teaching us that an augmentation is when two paired letters (in this case the "e" and "l") are used twice, but where there is an intervening sound between the second pair. That separation is the augmentation. The opposite (e.g., "early elm") is called diminution. The two terms, as applied to poetry (as opposed to music) were discovered by Kenneth Burke in his 1940 essay, "Musicality in Verse: As Illustrated by Some Lines of Coleridge."

Getting back to my sapling, I still had to fix the title. I thought about "Young Elm in Early April," but ultimately decided to forgo the augmentation and change the species of the tree, which I believe has even stronger sound value, being virtually an internal rhyme. Hence, it is now, "Young Maple in Early April." Whoa! Do the "pl" in Maple and the "pril" in April constitute an augmentation? Why, I believe they do. I also believe, although since I am writing this in October, I can't really check, that maple buds look more like ladybugs than do elm buds.

Finally, I thought I should give at least a nod to the late, great Richard Wilbur, whose work I have always admired for its sublime simplicity and for his daring to stand for stylistic tradition when all around him were demanding free-range revolution. One of his finest poems, "Exeunt," which movingly describes the melancholy of autumn, ends with the lines "A cricket like a dwindled hearse/Crawls from the dry grass." I do not believe I borrowed the word "crawl" from him, moving the setting from fall to spring in so doing transforming the imagined insect to a symbol of rebirth and not death, but I can't be 100 percent sure. In any event, when I look at the two poems side-by-side now, the symmetry astonishes me. It was never my intent. His is certainly the better of the two, by a significant margin. But I can live with that.

EXUENT
Richard Wilbur

YOUNG MAPLE IN EARLY APRIL
Jay Bryant

Piecemeal the summer dies;
At the field's edge a daisy lives alone;
A last shawl of burning lies
On a gray field-stone.

Bravely upward the sapling thrusts
Its skeleton bared for all to see.
While the warming fogs caress its limbs
And they shudder gratefully.

All cries are thin and terse;
The field has droned the summer's
final mass;
A cricket like a dwindled hearse-
Crawls from the dry grass.

Deep in the earth, its fare to seek
The insatiable life-root digs.
And the leaf buds crawl like ladybugs
Along the awakening twigs.

Perhaps this long diversion will strike you as excessively pedantic, like the first chapter of the textbook which Robin Williams instructs the students to rip out in *Dead Poets Society*, but if any of you are at all interested in the mental processes a writer actually goes through in plying his trade, this is a pretty good case study in how at least this one does.

I have never been brave enough to claim to be a really good poet. The closest I've come is in two statements: Once, while I was still in college, I bragged that at the age of twenty, I was as good a poet as John Keats was at the age of twenty. At twenty-one, of course, he zoomed past me like a moon-bound rocket, and by twenty-five, when he died, he had compiled a body of work that places him in the GOAT discussion. The other statement was made in 1985. When I announced that I would not write any more Christmas poems, I stated in public that "in the history of the world, no one else has ever written twenty good poems on the same subject." In truth, not all twenty of them were that good. But, anyway, I was out of Yuletide ideas.

(I think second place on the list of most good poems on a single subject is held by T.S. Eliot. *Old Possum's Book of Practical Cats* contains fifteen poems, every one of them way better than anything I ever wrote. But he was T.S. Eliot for cripes sake.)

My favorite poet is actually Percy Bysshe Shelly, whose tour de force "The Cloud" (What is it with me and clouds?) is the source of the title of my novel *Earth and Water*. (The majestical final verse of "The Cloud" begins:

I am the daughter of earth and water
And the nursling of the sky.
I pass through the pores of the ocean and shores
I change, but I cannot die....)

My God, what magnificent poetry that is. I don't think anyone in my lifetime has done it as well. The modern world is much the worse for the paucity of excellent poetry it has produced, and whether or not I did much to raise the average, at least I tried.

Good, bad, or mediocre, these poems really do represent what I was thinking about at various times over the six decades. Oddly, although for most of that time I was making my living in the political/governmental world, none of them has anything in particular to do with politics or public policy. I count this as a real strength of the book. Far too much art has been politicized during those decades, and I have no interest in adding to that unfortunate trend.

The eleven prose pieces (nine essays and two short stories) were all written as Christmas messages, but are, in most cases, not on an overtly Christmas theme. Pride of place goes perhaps to "Archipelago," upon reading which my dear friend, Dr. John Weicher, pronounced me a "world class" essayist, and my cousin Marilyn teased, "You're starting to get the hang of this."

For a writer who has wallowed for more than half a century in virtual obscurity, a little flattery will get you pretty much anything.

Hillsborough, North Carolina, 2023

I.

POETRY

ON THE MARRIAGE OF ONE'S DAUGHTER

For I was not the shadow of the bird
But more the cock; each morning I was heard
To call the sun from under sugar-cured
And ripening meadows, where the corn, interred
Each year would rise again, for it was lured
By gentle rain, a mother's tear, insured
Still further by the sun, which got its word
From me, the cock, the king of flock and herd.

A wee slip, cowslip, rose-lipt lass of ten,
You romped beneath the oaks, and ran from hens,
And hid beneath the divan in the den
When came to call the neighbor boy; he'd sense
That you were hiding, and so once again
I'd send him cookied off, on some pretense.
I knew you weren't for him, yes, even then
I'd entertain him knowing you were meant
To live a life not like your mother's, spent
With me. You would know finer men.

And so today at twenty-four, you glide
Up to the man so nervous there beside
Yourself, all rainbow-colored and dry eyed.
And if, all morning long, your mother cried,
It's only that a bit of her has died.
But like the corn, that bit's reborn inside
You, child; you, bride.

1963

ABOUT THE POEM

For many years, indeed decades, this was the favorite of my poems among the small circle of friends and family who knew anything about my work in verse. It was written in 1963, as a class assignment in an advanced poetry course. The professor expressed amazement that such a young person (I was nineteen or twenty) could have written it, given the point of view. It was my feeling then and is now that he was never convinced that I had not plagiarized it.

To the best of my knowledge, neither he nor anyone else who has ever read it has gotten the literary allusion in the first line, which comes, as does the meter, from Vladimir Nabokov's *Pale Fire*, to my mind one of the consummate creative works of literature of the twentieth century. The first two lines of *Pale Fire* read: "I was the shadow of the waxwing slain/By the false azure of the windowpane." For me, Nabokov's great book is a discussion of the nature of reality. In "On the Marriage..." I wanted to write something on very solid ground, very real. So I was not the shadow of the bird.

The rhyme scheme of this poem always draws attention and did from Dr. Nethercott on the day it was presented to the class. Each of the stanzas is built on a single rhyme, a device I would not return to for more than thirty-five years, when I used it less spectacularly in "The Imperative of Teleology." What I should have said, when he commented, somewhat disparagingly, on it, was to ask if he had ever seen anything like it. When he said no, I should have replied, "Good, then I did something original. I felt that if I was going to write a poem criticizing Nabokov, it should have at least one thing original in it." That would have started a discussion of Nabokov which surely would have convinced him I had in fact written the poem. And I wouldn't have had to embarrass him by asking point blank if he had understood it.

I also should have pointed out that while I certainly did not have the experience of being a father of the bride, I was raised on a farm and most of the imagery in the poem is farm imagery, whereas the wedding stuff might have been written by anyone who had ever attended a wedding, in any capacity.

THE DAY AFTER THE SOLSTICE

Halfway to the cold death of the universe. Today.
Counting down from the Planck length to the last instant
When the last string is freed to float alone in the chaos.
The last string of the last quark of the last proton.
Absolute zero. Four sixty below.
The end of time.

Then, mirabile dictu, in the very nick,
Like reunited lovers, two strings cling
And their passion is the turning point
That starts their climb up the longest hill,
Like Ike and Athena, or Jack and Jill
Or Sisyphus.

Every moment is warmer, the arrow flies toward its nock.
Eleven follows twelve. Tock-tick, tock-tick, tock.
The Hubble shifts toward blue and the cock
Crows at sunset, "Dos-toy-effa-SKI!"
The countup from zero to thirty billion proceeds.
Relentlessly.

And when the halfway point is reached once more
June twenty is not the day before, but after, the solstice.
And the world will be just like today.
For an instant just like today.
And I will again be eighty, and well on my way
To infancy.

2023

ABOUT THE POEM

This is the newest of the poems. I woke up in the middle of the night a few months ago with the idea for it in my mind and couldn't get back to sleep without getting up and going to my home office to flesh the whole thing out. I had been reading many books on cosmology in researching *God's Doctoral Thesis*, which will, I hope, be finished sometime soon.

The science behind the poetry is the notion that the universe might, if it contains enough mass, sort of bounce back after it reaches the end of its expansion and start contracting until it once again reaches the density that caused the Big Bang in the first place. If so, they say, time will literally run backward during the whole trip.

Of course, that also suggests that it could have happened any number (including an infinite number) of times already, with many, many more to yet come. Bouncy, bouncy, bouncy, repeat.

If you have never heard of Ike and Athena, you could read *Warped Passages*, by Dr. Lisa Randall, world-renowned cosmologist who holds an endowed chair at Harvard. I assume you know who Jack, Jill, and Sisyphus are.

11

I MIGHT HAVE MISSED ALL THE WONDERFUL THINGS

The last day I was thirty-nine,
I sat in the shade at Makaha
And watched a green lizard scurry under the croton.
I wanted to stay forever,
But I had to go home for my birthday party.

But I might have stayed
And missed the party
And all the wonderful things that have been since then.
And people would say,
"Whatever happened to Jay?"
And someone would answer, "he blew it all away
And became a bum."

Later we went to the North Shore
And I wanted to swim in the big surf
But the waves were too high and the beaches were closed.
But I might have gone in
And been caught by the big kahuna
And swept out to sea, nigh on to Nauru
(Where the natives are all stinking rich
Because their island
Is covered by bird dung, which brings in big bucks.)
I might have been eaten by a shark.

And people would say,
"Whatever happened to Jay?"
And someone would answer, "he drowned one day
In '83 and missed the party
And all the wonderful things that have been since then."

1983

12

ABOUT THE POEM

My fortieth birthday marked a melancholy turning point in my view of myself. Until then, the easy early successes of my career had yielded an almost unbroken optimism. Afterwards, things were a struggle, and I came more and more to doubt myself. Susan and I took a Hawaiian vacation. Our departure was delayed for a day by a blizzard in Maryland. I wanted to tack on a makeup day at the end, but that extra day was my birthday, and unbeknownst to me, Susan had planned a gala party. Grumbling all the way, I came home. She always hated this poem, because she felt that somehow I fault her for cutting the vacation short. No, no, my love, planning the party and pulling it off was a wonderful thing for you to do.

The melancholy I associate with the period that began February 19, 1983, has nothing to do with Susan and everything to do with slamming, unprepared, up against middle age, self-doubt, recognition of mortality, financial worries, and all the other stupid psychological mind games men like me play at such moments in their lives.

To the reader, I say that if you sense that the "wonderful things" weren't really wonderful, you have not gotten it quite right. For all the un-wonderful things, there were many I would not trade for all the guano in Nauru.

This, then, is the poem of my mid-life crisis. But, Susan, it was you who were mainly responsible for all the wonderful things I would have missed if I had not come home for the party.

CHILD

At six, I dreamed I had a sister
Though I was an only child.
I called her ma'am; she called me mister.
Her eyes were green and wild.

We'd shout until we thought we'd burst
Our fragile, children's lungs—
We'd naked climb through pines and firs,
And touch each other's tongues.

Or else we'd sit for hours and hours
Beneath the apple tree
And pick the petals from daisy flowers
Till Mother called for me.

The scent of apple that is left
Outlives the apple tree
And, mingled with her virgin breath
Perfumes my memory.

Though many a quickened pulse I've known
And many a wondrous thrill
Yet there are times when I'm alone
I know I love her still.

Circa 1965

ABOUT THE POEM

I always wanted a sister, particularly an older sister. That was obviously impossible, so I had to fantasize one. I was pretty good at it, but in the end, a sister of fancy could not provide the one thing I really wanted, which was a person to explain to me about girls. I just couldn't figure them out. When I was in the first grade, and thus six, I confiscated a surplus heart-shaped box of candy from home and took it to school on Valentine's Day. I walked in the door and deposited it on the desk of a little girl named Eleanor. It was no use. Eleanor was a very practical woman and not about to sell her favors for a box of chocolates. No, indeed, she had her mind set on a boy named Billy, whose mother was the second-grade teacher. Candy is dandy, but the promise of an in with next year's teacher is like money in the bank.

Some readers have sensed a hint of incest in this poem, I suppose from the tongue-touching thing. What dirty minds they have. So what if we were up in the trees without our clothes on? She was just imaginary.

Nonetheless, childhood sexual fantasies are most assuredly real things, and they certainly pre-date the spread of modern mass communications, which so many people these days want to blame for everything bad. Who needs the internet when you can conjure up a fantasy sister with no help at all from cable TV, porno websites, or even a dirty magazine? Or sex education in the schools for that matter?

The original version of the poem did not contain the final verse, which I added quite a few years later, upon reflection which I could not have done in 1965.

In order to protect the reputation of Kay Parlin Laney, my "real" fantasy sister of those days, no, we never got naked or touched tongues, or shared any other erotic fantasies. I am, however, delighted to have reconnected with her two years ago after our almost simultaneous widowhoods. It has been much fun, and a great comfort to have her in my life again.

A LADY LOVED ME ONCE

A lady loved me once
And when I kissed her in the forest
Leaves and moss, a fragrant chorus,
Had a shining song to sing.
Senses fused to one
Golden hair was there to strum,
And our laughter smelled of Spring.

A lady left me once
And I tasted salty tears,
Heard a door slam, saw disgrace
On my adolescent face,
Having eyes, and nose, and ears
All in place.

Circa 1965

ABOUT THE POEM

This is a poem about young love and how it absolutely scrambles the senses. The lady in question was the sweetheart of my senior year in high school, in Simsbury, Connecticut. Her name was Ruth, and she was very beautiful. Near the end of the school year, in a screaming temper tantrum, she dumped me. (So did each of my three "serious" pre-Susan romances. And Susan, too, but she came back, as you will discover.) Ruth added insult to injury by showing up at the senior class picnic with the geekiest boy in the class. I was perhaps the second geekiest, but at least I was on the student council, editor of the yearbook, and on the basketball team, albeit strictly as a bench warmer.

My favorite teacher was Mr. Maher ("Ma-HAR, like in cigar," he informed us), who taught senior physics. Ruth was the only girl in the class, along with perhaps ten or a dozen boys. Day after day, Mr. Maher observed Ruth and me engaging in silly adolescent lovers' stuff, passing notes and whatnot, but because we never let it interfere with the hard work of learning Boyle's Law or Newton's Theory of Gravitation, he tolerated it without comment. Imagine my surprise then, when one day shortly after our breakup, he called me into his office, something he had never done before.

"I have observed," he began, physicist-like, "that you and Ruth seem no longer to be a couple, is that true?"

"I'm afraid so," I said, my eyes downcast.

"Well," he responded, "since you are my two favorite people, that makes me sad. I was wondering if there was anything I could do to help." I was flabbergasted—imagine a teacher saying a thing like that! Composing myself, I replied in the negative; there seemed no hope for a reconciliation, I told him. He looked genuinely sad. "Was she just not as good a girl as we thought?" he asked.

"Maybe not as old," I replied, and he nodded knowingly, puffing on his pipe.

We were dead wrong, of course. The temper tantrum she had thrown at me was not childish like I thought. It was an adult strategic move. I was going to college in Chicago. She was going to college in Boston. Our romance was not going to survive that. But if she had managed the breakup in a "we can still be friends" way, I would have taken every opportunity to keep the flame alive. Letters, phone calls, plans for us to get together at every break in the schedule. Like I did successfully with Susan fourteen years later. Ruthie felt she had to come down on me so hard I wouldn't even think of such things.

It took me years to figure that out, but I will never forget the teacher who was willing to go way out on a limb for the two of us. Mr. Maher, wherever you are, thank you for one of the most wonderful compliments I have ever in my life been paid.

AMY, IN A LIGHT GREEN BLANKET

Springtime, like a verdant cradle
Rocks the newborn year to sleep.
Drowsy summer days will dawdle
Adolescent dreams to keep
Through an adult autumn ripeness
Into winter's whitened deep.

Amy, in a light green blanket,
On the thirty-first of May,
Looked at Mom with eyes unseeing
Saying, "I was born today."
Saying, "I am one foot ten,
I am eight pounds nine."
Saying, "I am yours to cherish,
Just as you are mine."

Amy, in a light green blanket,
(No one dared buy blue or pink)
Gurgled onto Daddy's shoulder,
Took her bath in Mommy's sink,
Seemed to sense that time was fleeting,

Seemed to sense that she was late.
She had nearly missed the springtime.
Coming summer wouldn't wait.

Would her summertimes be peaceful?
Would she love the autumn rain?
Would she spend a springtime evening
Like her mother, filled with pain,
Pain of which she'd know the worth,
Joyous pain of giving birth?

Like a lazy eagle sweeping,
Like a duck upon a stream,
Life is circles, ever keeping
Nature's pattern, perfect, clean.

1968

20

ABOUT THE POEM

This is the only sloppy, sentimental poem in the book, so just deal with it. Besides, if a man cannot get a little sentimental upon the birth of his first child, what good is he? It is something that happens only once in a lifetime, and say what you will, it's pretty darned special.

Amy Elizabeth was born on the 31st of May 1968, and welcomed into our apartment in Elk Grove Village, Illinois, on June 2. Two nights later, Bobby Kennedy was assassinated, as Susan, her mother, and I watched in horror on our little black and white television. That year, we had already endured the Martin Luther King assassination and the riots that followed, in Chicago as elsewhere. Susan and I were working for Jim Brady on the Bob Dwyer for Lieutenant Governor campaign that spring, (See "The 1981 Christmas Train,") commuting to his headquarters in the LaSalle Hotel in downtown Chicago. When the riots started, Dwyer sent the very pregnant Susan and me home, as the rioters were headed toward the hotel, which did indeed suffer some damage. It was a chilling sight to drive out the John F. Kennedy Expressway (and his assassination was still fresh in our minds as well) and see armored National Guard vehicles positioned atop every overpass. In that tumultuous year, the riot-filled Democratic National Convention was yet to come, and once again Chicago would be the victim of mass violence.

Chilling as it all was, it inspired me to no poetry. Nor did it really occur to Susan and me that America would not weather the storm and return to normal. We were right, and thus fully justified in viewing little Amy's future in terms of time-honored joys and sorrows, and not in terms of some manner of national apocalypse. Nature's circles are not always pretty, but they circle nonetheless, and, if America's summer of 1968 was far from peaceful, Amy's was.

AMANDA'S PANDA

I went downtown today to get a panda for Amanda.
He and I rode home together on the train.
And when I looked into his gumdrop eyes, to my surprise,
I saw the future there, as plain as plain.

I saw that very night, the monthling child would chew the gumdrops
Not knowing panda eyes from Playtex nubbins.
And deeper looking saw the bear, some four years old, adored
By a girl who wouldn't dream without her cubbins.

At ten, the dog-eared Teddy (and the dog-eared Daddy, too)
Must share Amanda with her school, her bike, her friends, her cat—
And the last light that I saw was Ted and I alone together
Two old men up in the attic for a chat.

O there never was a gypsy with the gift of crystal gazing
Who said a sooth from grains of sand, a hand, or stains of brandy
Nor any Gallup pollster with his programs and predictions
Who showed the future clear as Mandy's pandy.

1978

ABOUT THE POEM

There is nothing really Christmassy about this poem, but it was the Christmas card for 1978, the year our younger daughter, Amanda, was born. I read it at her wedding ceremony, twenty-one years to the day later. Amanda wanted to be able to drink champagne legally on her wedding night but wasn't willing to wait a single day longer than necessary to do it. That was so her—always in a hurry. High school in three years, college the same, two kids of her own by the time she graduated from law school after just another three years...two-year-old Madelyn holding her hand, baby Mallik in her arms as she strode proudly across the stage to get her foolscap, stealing the show, to loud applause.

The actual panda, which she named Charley, eventually became dog-eared and superannuated, just as he had predicted. Me too, perhaps.

JESUS, TEACHER OF VIRTUE

Jesus, teacher of virtue
Teach me to know the path true.
Lord, I beseech you
Show me the way.
I am a lost lamb today.

Jesus, prophet of peace
I pass each day in strife.
I fight the sin, and if I slack,
Then guilt sets in.
Bring your balm to my life.

Jesus, savior of sinners
Save me from vain self-destruction
Lord, make me whole.
Lead me beside the still waters
Restore my soul.

Savior, Teacher, Prophet.

Jesus, healer of heartache
Heal me, help me I pray.
Lay your hand on me.

Healer, Teacher, Prophet, Savior.

1998

ABOUT THE POEM

One Sunday in 1998, a celebratory service was put on at the Capitol Hill United Methodist Church, of which Susan and I were members. The celebration was to honor the tenth anniversary of the great Rick Stockdale as organist and choirmaster. Susan, who was a member of the choir, was much involved in the planning, and so a few weeks before the event, she came to me and asked me if I would write the lyrics of a hymn which would be sung to the tune of "Sun and Moon," from the hit Broadway show, *Miss Saigon*. She explained the song was a great favorite of Rick's and that he had once opined that he wished someone would write a hymn to it. Of course, I could not refuse, but what a challenge it was. The music is very complex, and writing new lyrics for it was frustrating and difficult.

The real problem with the idea of a special celebration was that there was no way it could be carried off without at least some participation by the honoree himself. Rick was just that critical to any service in the CHUMCH. Nonetheless, they did more or less keep the secret until early Sunday morning, when the choir regularly practiced. Then they sprang the surprise and left Rick with no other choice than to oversee the whole thing, including, as the offertory hymn, "Jesus, Teacher of Virtue." (Music by Claude-Michel Schonberg, lyrics by Jay Bryant.) Although it suffered some from the minimal amount of practice it got, I think it came off pretty well.

The sheet music subsequently got lost, and I am eternally grateful to choir members at the time, Chuck Carr and Gale Munro, for finding a copy so it could be included in this anthology.

Alabama-born Stockdale, who died far too young just a few years later, was a true musical genius and also a consummate showman. When he was no more than a toddler, he used to come home from church with his parents and play all the hymns on his toy piano. A true prodigy. Just a few years later, he was producing the Miss Alabama pageant. He and I discussed seriously the possibility of writing a Broadway musical based on the love affair between Thomas Jefferson and his slave mistress Sally Hemmings. Her love song to him was to be called "My Pursuit of Happiness," while his to her was "I Belong to You." One of my great regrets is that we were not given enough time to bring the project to a conclusion. Near the end of his life, I asked him if he still thought about the show, and he replied, "Every day."

Given the power of the story, the success of period pieces such as *Hamilton* and Rick's prodigious talent, I remain convinced it would have been a hit.

AND THIS TOO SHALL PASS AWAY

When Miltiades had run his final run
And called the news, was cheered; but there was one
An old man, grizzled, wan and rank
with hunched-up shoulders and a breath that stank,
Who pushed up through the crowd and stood beside
The messenger from Marathon and cried:
"What proof have you?
How do we know we've won?"
And it was only then the young Greek died.

Died young and pure did that good-tiding crier
But not so the old wretch, who lived to sire
The sages who have now been willed the earth
To meekly run, till it be stripped of worth;
Run by their sad and gloomy horoscope
In deference to that ancient misanthrope.
No more do fat clouds echo back the fire
Of strong and many athletes shouting hope.

One day to Rutland came a young man clad
In Grecian garb; he smiled and sang, and gladly
Striding to the bandstand in the square
Called to the townsfolk who assembled there:
"Fear not! The battle we have fought is won;
Our way of life, our nation shall go on."
And all the townsfolk jeered and called him mad
And thought he was a strange
phenomenon.

But one old man the town had long forgot
Pushed to the lad, and there beseeched him not
Stop talking, but continue with his news;
And so he did, amid the jeers and boos.
The folks began to mock the silly sight
Then, from a cloud o'erhead, a flash of light!
And rose the youth on skyward from that spot
And the old man spat, and murmured,
"Right, just right."

Circa 1963

ABOUT THE POEM

"And This Too Shall Pass Away" was at one point inserted into my novel, *Earth and Water*, as having been written by Ezra Ricker, poet, politician, and resident wise man of the town of Rutland, Maine, but taken out in the final manuscript. It was however composed at about the same time I wrote the first version of the novel, then entitled *The Thunderstorms*, in the middle sixties. ("His title stinks," wrote Alice Cromie in a generally encouraging appraisal, in which she said I reminded her of John Cheever. She was a real-life literary reviewer and the wife of Bob Cromie, host of the nationally syndicated "Book Beat" television program, and her willingness to read the manuscript was an enormous confidence-builder for me. Fran Coughlin (see "A Christmas to Remember") got her to do it.)

I really like novels in which one of the characters is a poet. I've already mentioned Nabokov's *Pale Fire*, and another example would be *Dr. Zhivago*, by Boris Pasternak. Is it only Russians who can combine the two literary forms? Perhaps they at least have done it best. And the Russian talent for combining art forms doesn't involve only literature, either. It was the great composer Modest Mussorgsky who composed "Pictures at an Exhibition," perhaps my favorite work of classical music.

Russian literature was a powerful influence on me in the days of my youth, although I never learned the language, and have always had to rely on translations. (Nabokov, of course, wrote some of his works in Russian and some in English; I find bilingual talent like his, Joseph Conrad's, and George Luis Borges's to be nothing short of astonishing.)

It is now stoutly maintained that the name of the famous messenger from Marathon was not in fact Miltiades, who was instead the commander of the Athenian forces, but rather Pheidippides, a trained runner sent by Miltiades. However, in the 1960s you could find sources which gave Miltiades himself as the name of the runner, so that's the way I wrote it.

THE IMPERATIVE OF TELEOLOGY

In the beginning, the word was true
And the biggest bang that ever blew
Fired up the stars and me and you
And the midnight owl that asks us who.

Keats found truth in an ancient vase
Teresa in a starving face
And Einstein's nub of chalk could trace
The line from here to outer space.

The judge wants whole and nothing but.
God's honest is from that a cut
Above. Is it the real nut?
Or superstitious scuttlebutt.

Is it eye for eye and tooth for tooth
Or when a seer says a sooth
Or Sherlock or some other sleuth
Deduces it? Has he found truth?

There is no truth says dour Camus
Which if it's true cannot be true
We are creation's residue
The truth is what we're here to do.

Circa 2000

ABOUT THE POEM

"The Imperative of Teleology" was written in 1998 and submitted for publication in an anthology called *Star Dust in the Morning*. This is one of those commercial operations that makes money by selling books to the authors. Although you don't have to buy to be published, the company behind it all, the International Society of Poets, is basically a very sophisticated direct marketing operation which plays on the intense desire of people like me to see their works in print.

They offer a few small prizes to a handful of the "best" poems submitted as a further incentive. I didn't win one of the prizes, just the publication itself, but I was very interested to read the poems that did win. They were good poems, universally heavy on intense descriptive lyricism. None of them dealt with anything approaching an original idea, but then, perhaps "The Imperative of Teleology" didn't either, as the nature of truth is hardly a new topic for discussion.

But it was a topical topic for discussion in 1998, the year of the Clinton impeachment, when the question of telling the truth—and whether it is important to do so—was front page news. Personally, I have long been entranced by the subtleties of this question, and this poem represents the best thinking I have been able to do on it. Truth is that which accords to the purpose of the universe, I think. So, if there is any truth at all, then the universe must have a purpose, hence teleology is imperative.

Although this is in no way a Christmas poem, Susan and I did send it out with our 1998 Christmas card, and a number of people have told me that they have kept it permanently on hand and look at it from time to time. That makes me feel good.

THE SCREECHING SHRILL STACCATO

The screeching shrill staccato of the times,
A mindless, programmed catalog of crimes
Disturbs my sleep, and makes me weep, till hoarse
My mind, imprisoned in a field of force,
Electricly forbidden to make rhymes,
Or love, and having never a recourse.

Where is the carefree kid who once was me?
Has he been tossed out, with the sad debris
A stapled, spindled, mutilated card,
His cybernetic id forever scarred
And turned into a homeless refugee
Skulking by the trashcans in the yard?

Carefree I was, but I was caring too
And most of all, my darling, cared for you.
And I could leave 'em laughing with a word
Or stun them with a thought they'd never heard.
Whatever was appropriate, I'd do.
Whatever thing was needed, I procured.

I cannot seem to get it right today
I've gotten palsy; my tongue won't obey.
Besides, the phrase, in Fortran, isn't clear;
The English have a word for it, I hear—
An epithet which keeps the ergs at bay
And serves to exorcise the engineer.

I've crawled into the trash can to survive
And none can get me here, here I will thrive.
I eat what they throw in here with a clink
I think I'm happy; then again I think
I'm miserable, just about alive
And just about destroyed by all the stink.

I need your help; I need it desperately
I need to know there's still a chance for me.
I need to stand up straight; I need to cope
And only you can help me, help me grope
Until, deprogrammed, I again can see
The wild, unreasoned madness that is hope.

1975

ABOUT THE POEM

This poem was written in 1975, which was a very bad year for me. I had lost out on the job I wanted, which went to Buddy Bishop, whom at the time I didn't know. Our great friendship and business partnership was still in the future. As a result, I went to work for Congressman Bob Michel in the Minority Whip's office of the House of Representatives. I was never happy in that job, in spite of the best efforts of Bob and his top aide Ralph Vinovich, both of whom are among the finest people I ever knew.

But the big problem was that Susan and I broke up. She took Amy and moved from our home in Maryland to Joliet, Illinois. I was devastated, humiliated, and mostly very lonely. The details would either bore you or not, and fearful of either reaction, I shall skip over them here. After three months of separation, Susan decided she had made a mistake and returned, but our relationship was tense, difficult, and altogether unsatisfactory for the remainder of the year and the first half of the next, filled with shouting, crying, and countless sessions at the marriage counselor's office. That it somehow survived and eventually achieved a breakthrough is little short of miraculous.

My sour mood resulted in a longing for the good old days, and it was an easy matter to associate my discontent with the general dehumanization of society which was everywhere apparent and being commented upon. I was desperately seeking Susan, not just in the house, but in the warmth of a loving companionship, nurtured by which I could once again face the world with the calm and confidence I had always counted on. It would happen; the screeching, shrill staccato would end, but it was a close-run thing, as Wellington said about Waterloo, and I think this poem shows just how critical it was to my sanity.

VEAL

And I saw Trotsky chatting with Rush Limbaugh
As they shuffled ahead in the amorphous line
Toward the station where the cattle cars stood.
The beginning of the line was somewhere over the horizon.

There were men in togas and saffron-colored robes.
Loincloths and leather jerkins
Breeches and hose, business suits and blue jeans.
All the oppressors of all time.

Mendelsohn and Pindar,
Marlowe and Pat Boone,
Mencius and Shaka Zulu.

Burly Amazons in tight leather jackets kept order.
They had red lips and black whips.

Overlooking it all, from the top of the marble steps
Stood the professor, smiling as she watched the men board the cattle cars.
Roll up, fill up, roll away. Again.

Heloise appeared from nowhere,
Ran up and down the line, calling for Abelard.
"Kill that man-loving bitch traitor," shouted the professor.
And one of the guards did.

"Strange," the Nazarene said to me as he shuffled along with the rest of us.
"What does death really mean today?"

2018

ABOUT THE POEM

I suppose this poem will cause much consternation among my female readers, friends, and relatives. For that reason, I hesitated to include it in this collection. But I decided that not to include it would be cowardly.

I am not, I insist, anti-feminist. I believe the changed role of women is the most important sociological development of my lifetime, and I believe there are still remnants of past discrimination that need to be corrected in our society and even more so in others, especially Islam.

But there is an extreme faction on the left end of the bell curve of feminism that is occupied by true man-haters, and I shudder to think what could happen if they ever got control. A matriarchy run by this faction would be much worse than any patriarchy has ever been, or could be, for the simple reason that men need women, but women do not need men. With modern technology, even less than before.

"A Woman Needs a Man Like a Fish Needs a Bicycle," reads the bumper sticker. On our dairy farm, the boy-calves were fattened and sent off to the butcher. The heifers were allowed to grow up and lead a normal cow's life. In the old days, one bull could service a whole herd. Nowadays, with artificial insemination, he can service many herds, although it is, I suppose, not as much fun for either gender.

"Veal" is, of course, a fantasy. No doubt it will never be possible to line up the dead with the living. They would have to be simply cancelled, erased. But is it possible to imagine a world where men are packed into cattle cars and shipped off to death chambers of one kind or another? Before the horrors of the twentieth century, people might not have believed it was. But now we know otherwise, and must answer:

Yes, it is.

LOCAL WEATHER

It was a bright September morning, nine eleven.
But there was local weather near the tomb
Where the men flew down and down and down to heaven
Through the gloom.

2002

ABOUT THE POEM

If you are too young to remember the live coverage of the 9/11 event, it will be difficult for you to get the full impact of the poem because I believe the tragedy of the World Towers jumpers has been almost completely eliminated in the various remembrances of that horrific day. The people who produce such things apparently don't think the public can bear the thought of it. They may very well be right, but for me, it is the ultimate horror of the event, and I wanted to commemorate their martyrdom. Re-reading the little poem, I realize that I, too, pulled back from a more graphic presentation. I did not, for example, use the word "plop" a sound heard in the background every few seconds during the coverage before the buildings' collapse.

QUANTUM PHISICS

The universe splintered asunder
When Adam was 5-5-8-4
And the Beagle sank suddenly under
A gale off Galapagos' shore.
And it happened again when your mother
Died on the day you were born,
And a second ago when another
Proton from its atom was shorn.

By now, ten to the eighty-ninth power
Have gone to their own separate doom
As billions split off every hour
And Heisenberg laughs in his tomb.
In some, you were very unlucky
And died in a seven-car wreck;
In others you're King of Kentucky
At war with the King of Quebec.

The many-worlds interpretation
Is one of the elegant ways
That Schrödinger's feline equation
Is solved in smart Princeton cafés.
But maybe there only is one world
One grand spacetime implicate order
One hologram universe unfurled
Like ink in a glycerin mortar.

The pestle of time swirls the mixture
And memory smears and grows faint
And there can be no solid fixture—
The whole is the only restraint.
Each boy is each butterfly's brother
The explicate but a facade
Behind which we're one with another
And all joined together are God.

ABOUT THE POEM

The fact that physicist David Bohm might be right in his interpretation of quantum theory used to upset me a great deal, because it was bruited about by various authors that he and he alone among the quantum fraternity had abolished the free will factor which Heisenberg and the others had triumphantly made scientifically respectable—indeed imperative—again, after Newton, Darwin, and Einstein had banished it to the slums. For me, free will is the core of all worth in living.

But a closer reading of Bohm convinced me that his "implicate order" theory allows free will to escape unscathed. So do all the other competing explanations for the undeniable, but oh, so mysterious quantum phenomena, including Hugh Everett's "many worlds" theory, made famous (with only moderate poetic license) by Tom Clancy in his 1999 novel *Timeline*, and the 2003 movie of the same name.

"Quantum Physics" is my first poem of the new millennium and was inspired by my old college chum, Ed Smith, who called me out of the blue after thiry-six years. It turns out that he, like me, has found great intellectual stimulation from reading about quantum theory, which he reports was unmentioned in his Northwestern physics classes. (I took no college physics, believe me, and knew nothing about quantum theory until I read John Gribben's *In Search of Schrödinger's Cat* while on vacation in St. Thomas in 1984.)

It long remained a mystery to me why this immensely important subject was not given the popular attention that Einstein's theories had, as it is far more important and interesting. But I actually think that due to Clancy and others, it has largely caught up in the new century. Bohm, on the other hand, seems to have largely been forgotten, which is a pity. That is changing, I believe, due to the growing popularity and acceptance of string theory, to which you have been introduced already in "The Day After the Solstice."

STAVROS'S CRUISE

Somewhere
In mid-linguistic air
Somewhere
Between indecipherable Olde English
And binary code,
Between odd rap and rapt ode,
Lies the mother lode
Of language.

And in that versatile vehicle
You can fly or burrow
Or turn a furrow,
Exposing the fertile soil to the air
And the seeds
Of Truth.
Weeds
Will also grow
But can you know
The difference?
(Consider the lowly dandelion.
Does its blossom not compare
With prized coreopsis?)
So where, John, where
Is Truth?
I need to know: am I
Bespectacled, bald and fat
With spaces between my teeth
A Lie?

The pretty girl at the party
Would not eat the venison –
Would not be
An accessory
To the murder of the deer; she
Took the turkey.
And I made her cry
When I looked in her eye
And asked if only beauty
Deserved not to die.

Stavros admired the fine china
On the luxury liner,
While Black Walter, the waiter
Served shrimp with tomato.
Later,
Stavros watched the lights of Gibraltar
Disappear into the black water,
And raising his gaze to the Pleiades
Contemplated Archimedes.

Circa 1999

ABOUT THE POEM

This poem is so abstruse and difficult that sometimes I wonder about it. But even more often, I wonder *at* it. It was written in 1998, about the same time as "The Imperative of Teleology," and is more or less on the same subject. Keats makes an appearance here, too.

But the real wonder of this poem is the hilarious (to me, anyway) final stanza. Has anyone ever purposefully put together so many "bold, bad rhymes"? China rhymes with liner? Not even in Maine, where the two words would be pronounced chiner and linah. So, can he be serious, you ask? No, as soon becomes obvious. Black water is rhymed (?) with Gibraltar, and must not be confused with Black Walter, which *would* rhyme with Gibraltar. Walter, however, is the waiter, and waiter is rhymed with tomato, which you are expressly invited to pronounce tomater, particularly as the next word is later. And to cap it off, Pleiades is ridiculously rhymed with Archimedes, author of the famous treatise on…wait for it… FLOATING BODIES! Please tell me you think all that is funny.

Then ponder the Overwhelming Question. Is Stavros still on the ship at the end of the poem? Or has he thrown himself overboard, into the black water, from which, and into which, he observes Gibraltar sink? Is he himself, and not the ship, the floating body? Ah, ambiguity, more delicious than shrimp with tomater.

Stavros is, of course, a Greek on an ocean journey (as opposed to an ode on a Grecian urny*), so we are back to Keats and the nature of truth. If Stavros is in the water and drowns, and his body is recovered, he might wind up cold on a Grecian gurney. What a versatile vehicle language is!

I have given a number of poetry readings over the years but have never read this one, because, frankly, it is impossible to read aloud; it must be presented in print to be understood.

By the way, the incident about the venison is real, more or less, and happened in the early 1980s. I felt bad about making the poor girl cry, but not too bad.

*Not to confused with Stavros's buddy Earnesto, or, as he is called, Grecian Ernie.

DON'T PUT CHEESE ON PEAS

Don't put cheese on peas.
The flavor doesn't please.
You can eat peas
In your dungarees,
Your best tuxedo or your BVD's
But please do not put cheese
On peas.

I've dined in the finest restaurants
From Paris to Belize.
And among their recipes
For meats and beets and
Sweet pommes frites
And treats replete with calories
I was never proffered peas
In cheese.

Two Krafty Viennese
Tried pepper jack on peas
But it made them sneeze
So they had to cease
So they tried some cheddar
But it worked no better
And today they're devotees
Of the maxim don't mix cheese
And peas.

Your uncle Ebeneez
That marvelous old tease
Once munched some muenster
On his water skis
But he kept his peas
In his old deep freeze
And he never once ate cheese
With peas.

Monkeys eat peas in trees
And monks while on their knees.
But all the priests
And chimpanzees
From Borneo to the Peloponnese
Would rather fast than feast on peas
With cheese.

A lady named Louise
Squeezed brie on broccolis.
She loved ricotta
On sliced tomatta
And smoky gouda
With the freshest fruitta
But she eschewed chewing cheese
And peas.

So, children:

Learn your ABC's
And mind your q's and p's.
But as you live
Your whole life through
There's just one thing
You must never do
Please, please, I beg you please
Do not put cheese
On peas.

2014

ABOUT THE POEM

I thought a bit of comic relief was appropriate somewhere on these pages, so I am including "Don't Put Cheese on Peas," just for grins.

The premiere recitation of this poem was performed to raucous laughter at the famous Luna Café in downtown Raleigh before a packed house of public officials and community leaders in June 2014. It is also believed to be the only poem ever officially recorded by the Wake County Office of the Registrar of Deeds, where it never fails to startle the real estate agents and settlement attorneys who happen across it.

PROPOSAL IN WINTER, WITH STRINGS

Started the evening in three-quarter time
Hopes were as high as the strain
Of violin solo, with cello behind.
Hope was ill fated, and pain
Was to come when the rhythm
Disrupted itself.
Anarchy reigned.

No was the answer, and gone was the chance
That life could be waltzed through, as if one were prancing
In time to a drummer's controlling clip-clops.
No is a snowstorm that drops
Dampness and cold on my shoulders:
Somehow the hurt never stops.

1965

ABOUT THE POEM

The thousands of beautiful girls at Northwestern always seemed as out of reach to me as so many Hollywood starlets. The first date I had went badly, and I retreated into a social shell. That all changed one fine spring afternoon when I walked into a campus meeting and beheld Kaaren across the room. I had never before, nor have I ever since, fallen in love at first sight, but I did that day. I simply had to make a play for her.

So I did. I took her to a fancy Chicago restaurant for dinner. We both attended a convention in Indianapolis, and we ate lunch together at a coffee shop counter in the old Harrison hotel there. We must have been acting a little mooney, because an old woman walked up to us and said, "Now, don't you two run off and get married too young!" We giggled and promised her we wouldn't; to my mind, though, it was settled. Surely that old woman, like a kindly version of the Mac-Beth witches, was sent by the Author of our drama to predict the final scene.

Kaaren and I dated regularly for two years, never exactly going steady, but nonetheless each other's normal companion at fraternity and sorority parties, study dates, and all the other social events that make up undergraduate extra-curricular life. Eventually, though, I could see that she was becoming bored by the lack of excitement in our relationship.

She was a year ahead of me, and as her graduation approached, it seemed to me that she was becoming more distant. Then one night I asked her to marry me. She didn't just say no, she said hell, no. Her exact words were, "I just can't picture myself waking up next to you every morning."

The conversation took place on the sidewalk on the corner of Sheridan Road and Emerson Street, just a few steps from where it had all begun. I walked back up Sheridan Road to Zeta Psi. And, yes, it was snowing.

The good news is that marrying Kaaren would have been a terrible mistake; it could never have lasted. The next year I met Susan, and that one, for all its tribulations, lasted for fifty-four years, until her sad death did us part.

CHRISTMAS MOON

The ornamental Christmas moon
Is hung on Heaven's lowest limb,
And listens to the gentle tune
Of the joyous Christmas hymn.

Reflecting in her pearly light
And on her sonar ear
Every detail of the night
Every evening of the year.

Every earthrise since time's dawn
On the wax and on the wane
Seeing nighttime's story drawn
Over mountain, sea, and plain.

Resting army, nightingale,
Sentry, drunk, and furtive bat—
Silent ship and siren's wail.
Lover, owl, and alley cat.

Once a stable, in tableau
With a star out in the east;
Three on camels toward the glow
Shepherds bringing lambs unfleeced.

Then again, Gethsemane
And every evening since
She waits, ever patiently
The next arriving savior-prince.

1974

ABOUT THE POEM

In the foreword, I mentioned my Christmas poem era—1966–1985. About half of these were humorous and half were serious. I am including a few of the serious ones here, not because there weren't any good humorous ones, but because they tended to be topical in the year they were written, and by now, the humor will be lost on all but a very few folks still alive. You would have to be both an octogenarian and have enough wits left to remember such things as the New York City bankruptcy scare of 1975. I did a really funny one on that. But "Christmas Moon," written the year before, in 1974, is as evergreen as a poem can be. I put it on my Facebook page last year, and it was quite well received by those who read it. I hope you like it, too.

CHRISTMAS, LIKE A FERTILE VALLEY

Christmas, like a fertile valley
Beckons those who, terrified
Walked the year's dry, barren desert,
Climbed the craggy great divide.

Christmas, we can stay a moment
But we then must hurry on
Next year beckons like a passage
Unseen yet through not-quite dawn.

Pioneer or eastern king,
Shining star or smell of gold
Where shall we go after Christmas?
Toward a destiny untold.

Christmas, like a fertile valley.
Beckons those who, sanctified,
Walked the year's dry, barren desert,
Climbed the craggy great divide.
Never, ever, lost their pride.

1972

ABOUT THE POEM

Nineteen seventy-two was a very difficult year for me. I was an assistant to the Governor of Illinois, the fondly remembered Richard B. Ogilvie. He was up for reelection that year and started off way, way behind as a result of having initiated a desperately needed but enormously unpopular state income tax. Those of us on the Ogilvie team, and he himself, worked our butts off and ran an amazing campaign. After trailing by more than twenty points early on, we lost by a mere 1.8%. But losing is losing, and I was out of a job. This Christmas poem is dedicated to all those who labored in the trenches in that campaign and to anyone who has ever had to find peace and solace in the Christmas season after a tough year.

THE 1981 CHRISTMAS TRAIN

FOR JSB, *il miglior fabbro.*

I.

Illinois Central Railroad
Clackin' on down the line
Packin' a heavy mail load
'Cause it's comin-on Christmas time.

II.

Got a circus bear in the baggage car and he's half-gassed;
Got a whole coach for the press, all sitting down;
Got one car full of doctors needing bills passed;
And another full of docs in mask and gown.
This train is life, and where it's been is memory
With happiness and pain at either end.
For on some crowded platform lurks an enemy
And on some lonely platform waits a friend.

III.

Down through Egypt our Express speeds
Past Centralia and DuQuoin.
In the bar, tell "Bishop Gillespie,"
In the diner, "Flame-in-the-boin."
Wave to Pino Castelleri
Ain't got time to stop the train.
Wave to Don and Jack and Perry
And the Jones campaign.

IV.

Train that's bound for glory
Clackin' on round the bend.
Flakkin' this year's Christmas story:
Brady's on the mend.

1981

ABOUT THE POEM

John Hinckley fired six bullets in about two-and-a-half seconds in his March 30, 1981, attempt to assassinate President Ronald Reagan. The first one hit Press Secretary Jim Brady in the head, just above his left eye, leaving him partially paralyzed and causing his eventual death on August 4, 2014. Jim had been a friend of Susan's and mine since the mid-sixties and was the person as responsible as anyone for starting our careers in politics and government. One frigid January day in 1968, the phone rang in our Old Town, Maine, apartment. She answered. He asked her if the two of us would be willing to come back to Illinois and work for him on the Dwyer for Lieutenant Governor campaign. Susan was four months pregnant, cold, and miserable. She had had it with Maine.

"You'll have to talk to Jay about it," she said to him. "I've got to start packing." So back to Illinois we went, and the rest, quite literally, is history.

On the fateful day, we were hurrying across Capitol Hill on our way home, listening to the assassination attempt reports on the radio. No one knew if it was part of an international conspiracy, or what. It was reported that Jim had been hit. Then that he had died. Then that he was not dead but only wounded, although seriously. It was a horrible, horrible day. By the fall, he was home and appeared to be getting better.

He was perhaps the most colorful person I ever met—the life of every party. He had a million stories, which he was continually obliged to tell, party after party. "Bishop Gillespie" was about an itinerant southern Illinois preacher/huckster. "Flame in the Boin" was a hilarious "Who's-on-First" type routine between a diner and a waiter. Jim accepted the nickname "Bear," but insisted that like Yogi, he was "smarter than the average bear." As Presidential Press Secretary, he brought order to raucous news conferences by insisting that the reporters remain seated throughout the sessions.

His father was a railroad man, and Jim never tired of expounding on the greatness of railroads. Fresh out of the University of Illinois, he had worked as a lobbyist for the Illinois Medical Society. Later, he managed Congressional campaigns. That stuff is all in the poem. "*Il Miglior Fabbro*," is, of course T.S. Eliot's tribute to Ezra Pound in "The Waste Land."

We had a delightful lunch with Jim in the White House sometime in the fall of 1982, but it was clear that he was not really improving. In his special van, he did make it to my surprise birthday party in 1983 (see "I Might Have Missed All the Wonderful Things" above.)

They broke the mold after they made Jim Brady.

CALL THE ROLLER

If Wallace Stevens had not lived
America would have more poets.
For all the men
Who might have been
But were persuaded to think that they,
Like he,
Could be and not be
Would have been,
Including me.

1966

ABOUT THE POEM

It is a great pity that so many of the poetic giants of the first half of the twentieth century have been forgotten, or at least marginalized. In Stevens's case, pretty much forgotten. I polled my children and grandchildren, as well as their spouses and significant others, and found not one of them knew who he was. The closest answer came from my eldest daughter, Amy. who, never wanting to miss the chance for a smartass remark, answered, "She was the Duchess of Windsor. Easy Peasy." I forgive her because in addition to her ever quick wit, she is an indefatigable Anglophile, who quickly adopted the sobriquet "The Princess Royal" for herself. My granddaughter Madelyn, answered that while neither she nor her husband, Jamie, knew the answer, she supposed that since it was me doing the asking, it was probably an author, and her mother, Amanda, promptly proclaimed her the winner, being "closest to the pin."

Of course, I don't know any of the great poets of their generations either, but there's a reason for that.

Wallace Stevens (1879–1955) was one of the very finest poets or his or any other era. His stuff was weird, highly abstract, and difficult to understand. But unforgettable. One of his most famous poems was "13 Ways of Looking at a Blackbird," one of which is: "A man and a woman are one/A man and a woman and a blackbird are one."

My favorite Stevens poem is "The Emperor of Ice Cream," which is about a funeral.

But for me, the real importance of Stevens is that he never made his living at poetry. He was an insurance company executive in Hartford, Connecticut. In 1966 or thereabouts, I wrote the lines above, which I subsequently entitled, "Call the Roller." (The first line of "The Emperor of Ice Cream" is, "Call the roller of big cigars…")

There are those who don't think Stevens was a truly "American" poet and seek to place him among the ex-pat poets of his generation, such as T.S. Eliot and Ezra Pound. Piffle. The most prominent of Stevens's biographers, Harvard's Helen Vendler, destroyed their thesis in a 2012 lecture at Stanford, which you can view on YouTube. But in her argument she does not bring up what for me is the coup de grace of the point, which is: what could be more American than an insurance company executive?

II.

PROSE FICTION

Arty, the Artificial Christmas Tree
2014

Arty, the artificial Christmas tree, felt as happy as a daffodil in April. It was only natural. Arty's life, after all, was very daffodillish. He spent most of the year hidden away in the dark, but then, for three glorious weeks, he got to come out into the fresh air and show everyone his colorful beauty, listen to their compliments, and puff up with pride.

Pop-Pop placed him carefully in his stand, smoothed out his branches, plugged in his pre-strung white lights, strung the big, bright colored lights he had bought for Arty just to make him extra special, and hung the crystal ornaments, the Wedgewood ornaments, the elegant White House ornaments, the puffy needlepointed Twelve-Days-of-Christmas ornaments, and placed the smiling angel on the very top.

He hooked the huge green ornament safely to a solid branch near Arty's trunk. A casual passer-by might not even notice, even though it was huge, because it was green, and blended in with Arty's needles, but Pop-Pop and Nana, and Zoe and Adrian, and the five grandchildren would look for it, because it was in remembrance of Grandma Saunders, Pop-Pop's own grandmother, long passed away but well known to the whole family by the stories Pop-Pop told of how special she had made his Christmases when he was a little boy like Jayden. (A few years ago, Pop-Pop would have said like Ryan, and before that, like Petey, but now it was Jayden's turn.)

Way back, more than a hundred years ago, when Grandma Saunders was a little girl, like Emma, she was given a huge green ornament as her one and only Christmas present, which she kept for seventy years and then gave it to Pop-Pop—much to the consternation of Uncle Herbie. For the next twenty-two years, he had hung it on the Christmas tree, but then, in 1996, tragedy struck, and he dropped it on the tile floor of the solarium in the house in Salem and smashed it to bits. Pop-Pop cried like a baby, and the grandchildren marveled to hear that when he told the story, as he always did, because they couldn't imagine Pop-Pop crying.

But for Christmas the next year, Zoe had given him a huge green ornament, and while it wasn't the same, it was still a family treasure, and now it was part of the story. Arty loved to hear the story as much as the grandchildren did, and he was proud to hold the grandma Saunders ornament, even though it was just a replica.

Arty stood, as he did every year, in front of the big picture window that faced the back yard. From there, he could see the Higgins' house, through a few bare limbed trees. It was a big house, with lots of glass, and Arty could see it was ablaze with lights. He hoped the Higgins family could see him, because otherwise, there was no one who could look in his window—a few squirrels, perhaps, and Pop-Pop if he went out onto the deck for some reason. In the December chill, no one else was likely to go out onto the deck, or into the backyard, not even Nana. Arty's whole thing was to be seen.

A Christmas tree has no other purpose, he thought, but to bring happiness by being seen. That was why he looked forward so much to when the grandchildren arrived. No one got more happiness from looking at Arty than they did. Jayden and Emma would look the closest, searching out every one of the Twelve-Days-of-Christmas ornaments. So he was shocked when Nana leaned on Pop-Pop's shoulder as they looked at him and said, somewhat sadly, "I guess we'll be the only people to see the decorations this year."

"Yes, but we'll have fun at Adrian and Chris's with all the kids there," Pop-Pop answered, trying to cheer her up; it worked, sort of, and Nana smiled. But Arty was uncheerable. No grandchildren. No Adrian and Chris. No Zoe and Phil. No audience for Arty. He felt like climbing back into his box. Then he had an even worse thought. No children meant no Santa. He would take their presents to Adrian and Chris's house. Santa was Arty's best friend, the only human who knew Arty was sentient. Santa always talked to him, while he ate the cookies the children left for him. But not this year.

Nana hadn't been completely right. The FedEx Ground man came by with a package from Aunt Carol, and he told Nana her tree looked beautiful. And of course, Wally and Audra from next door stopped in to exchange presents with Pop-Pop and Nana, and the four of them sat in the family room and chatted for a while. But that was about it, and as the days before Christmas went by, Arty grew more and more melancholy. Then, on the morning of the twenty-fourth, all was hustle and bustle as Nana and Pop-Pop packed up for the trip to Adrian and Chris's house in Smithington. They took all the presents from under Arty's branches, leaving him feeling almost naked.

Then they were gone, and the doors were locked behind them.

Christmas trees don't have tear ducts, but if they did, Arty would have soaked the round Christmas quilt Nana had made from a printed cotton fabric showing scenes from the stable in Bethlehem and carefully spread out around his base. The hours dragged on and on. Once a blue jay hopped up on the deck railing and looked at Arty, but it only made him feel lonelier. No one but a stupid blue jay will see me all Christmas Eve, he thought.

A cold, December night settled in.

Then, all of a sudden, up on the rooftop, there arose a clatter, startling Arty. It sounded like Santa, but how could that be? Didn't he realize the whole extended family was in Smithington? Of course. He must. Santa didn't make mistakes like that. What was going on?

In a twinkling, Santa stood in front of him. He was holding a bundle of some kind. A present? No, it was moving. A puppy? No, it was a baby! A tiny baby, wrapped in one of Santa's stocking caps.

Santa spoke hurriedly. "Arty, I need your help," he said. "I haven't got much time left and lots more to do. Look at her, Arty. Isn't she sweet? I found her on the Methodist Church step. She wouldn't have lasted the night out in the cold, but she'll be fine here. I need you to watch her and entertain her if she wakes up. I'll come back and get her after I'm done with my rounds.

He carefully pulled Nana's quilt out just a bit and positioned the baby on it, her sleeping face toward Arty. "If she wakes, she'll see your beautiful lights and ornaments," he said, "and she won't cry.

"Just do what you do, Arty," he said. And then he was gone.

For the next four hours, Arty watched the baby. Three times she awoke, whimpered briefly, and then, just like Santa had said, focused her tiny eyes on

Arty, smiled, and fell back asleep. It was almost dawn when Santa returned, appearing again, as if by magic, in the family room. He gathered up the bundled baby. "Mrs. Claus will know just what to do," he said. "Thank you, Arty." He started to go but then turned quickly and grinned at Arty. "By the way," he said. "You never looked better, old friend."

A few hours later, in Smithington, the pitter patter of tiny feet awoke the sleeping adults, who trundled downstairs to watch the excited children open their presents. But there was one present no one could explain. The card said it was for Nana and Pop-Pop, and when they opened it up, they found an astonishingly beautiful creche. The straw in the manger almost looked like spun gold, and the whole scene exuded a wonderful aroma, which on examination proved to be coming from some nuggets of resin in a small burlap bag marked with a strange word.

"Olibanum?" Zoe said. "I never heard of it."

"I can look it up," Petey said, fingering his new Christmas tablet. "Hmm," he said, "it's another name for frankincense."

"Wow," Pop-Pop said. "That's pretty authentic. What a wonderful present. Which one of you is it from?"

"It's from Santa," Emma said, and of course, no one would contradict her. "Here," she added, handing Nana the card. "It says so right on it."

Nana studied the card. "Well," she said finally, "I guess Emma's right. It's handwritten, and it says, 'Thank you. Sometimes people do good deeds without even knowing it. I hope you will display this next year somewhere near your Christmas tree.' And it's signed 'Santa Claus.'"

"What a pretty card," Adrian said, looking over her shoulder. "What is that Bible verse printed at the top?"

"Matthew 25:40," Nana read. "Verily I say unto thee, inasmuch as ye have done it unto one of the least of these, ye have done it unto me."

A Christmas Question
2003

"Why does Santa give rich kids more presents than poor kids?" the little girl asked. From the mouths of babes, her grandfather thought. Of course, she had no idea of the complexity of the question. He knew the answer, and he didn't want to take too long in telling it to her, for fear she would interpret his silence, though momentary, as confirmation of her worst fears.

That had happened to him before. In the most dramatic case, a businessman had asked a question on the telephone, a question for which the answer was far more complex than the man could have known. The grandfather, not yet a grandfather then, had hesitated, and the man had interjected, "I guess your silence tells me all I need to know." That was certainly wrong but it didn't matter. The man had hung up, and the grandfather knew he had lost a lot of money and a friend in those few seconds of hesitation.

"Because," he told the little girl, "Santa isn't dealing in things, really. He's dealing in happiness."

Her hesitation was not a problem. It gave him a chance to look down at her, at those huge incongruously blue eyes framed by all that dark hair. He sensed that behind those eyes a crew of highly specialized synapses was swinging into action for the first time, to unload and process a new concept, a thought sufficiently abstract to require their expert attention. Rookies at their job, they wanted to make sure they sent the right words tongueward.

She licked her upper lip, and the blue eyes squinted just a tiny fraction. "So, a poor kid," she said, explaining his answer, asking him, really, if she understood what he had said, "that got a pair of shoes would be as happy as a rich kid that got a hundred toys."

"More or less," the grandfather said.

"Okay," she said, turning away in her Christmas-dinner dress and skipping off in her patent-leather shoes, looking for cousins.

Later, alone in his basement office, the grandfather indulged himself in the thoughts he had wanted to think during the conversation but had stifled in order to pay attention to the moment, ever so much more important than sorting all the ideas out, more important because it involved her, with a lifetime yet to make something of it, and use it to influence the lives of others, by the dozens or millions, who knew? Whereas the sorting involved only him.

He was trying to draw a line, the Proper Indulgence of the Innocence of Youth Line.

"Feed the birds," Mary Poppins sang, "Tuppence a day." But the movie's ancient banker, presented as the very image of Scrooge, argued for investing the two pence in his bank, and catalogued the economic wonders that ensued from even a modest investment, the very amount, he cackled, that he had started with.

The grandfather didn't think of himself as a scroogy geezer, but he knew the old banker's argument was right, and that the birds would get by, whether the children fed them or not. But, of course, it wasn't really about the birds; it was about the children. Should one deny children an innocent pleasure in order to teach a lesson in economics? But yet again, if one did not teach children economics, would they grow up ignorant and vote for fatuous, sentimentalist economic policies that would wind up ruining the well-being of millions, as had been done in so many countries in his own lifetime?

And then a third turn of the line occurred to him. Was not the old woman selling the little two-pence packets of birdseed an entrepreneur, too, every bit as much as the equally superannuated banker?

Draw the line, Granddad, draw the line.

How much economics should a child be exposed to? How much violence? How much sex, on television and in school?

The word "overprotection" crawled to the top of his consciousness, and he pondered it. Today's parents, with their high-tech car seats and safety-tested toys protected their children physically, but what protection were they providing morally, spiritually, intellectually? They wanted to protect children from tasting failure, low self-esteem, and any sort of insult based on stereotype. He realized his line was zigzagging and took only small comfort from realizing that everyone else's was, too. The politically-correct lines zigged when his zagged, but was there a principle he could apply to show he was right and they were wrong? He was working on that problem when a call interrupted him.

"Come say goodbye, Granddad, they're leaving."

At the top of the stairs, a pair of blue eyes, fifty-five years older than the little girl's, but identical nonetheless, smiled at him. He put his arm around the girl's grandmother and together they waved good-bye as the next two generations drove away.

That evening, over turkey and mayonnaise sandwiches, he talked to her about Santa and happiness, and lines that zigzagged.

"You think too much," she told him. "We turned out okay, and they'll turn out okay. All things in their season, the good and the bad."

"How do you know?" he asked.

"Well," she said. "Once upon a time, there was this manger..."

III.

ESSAYS

A Christmas to Remember
2000

This is the story of the first of my twenty annual Christmas poems, the only one that was never printed as a Christmas card. It was also the first Christmas Susan and I spent together—1966.

It was a different world thirty-four years ago. It was the year both the Black Panthers and NOW were formed, and the year Mao-Tse tung (as we spelled it then) started the Cultural Revolution. The Department of the Interior issued the first endangered species list, Medicare began, and the Supreme Court handed down the Miranda ruling. In spite of all that, it was a great year for the Republicans; we picked up four seats in the Senate and 47 in the House. Susan and I helped.

The NFL season that year would lead to the first Super Bowl. Steve Spurrier won the Heisman Trophy and the Orioles swept the Dodgers in the World Series. *A Man for All Seasons* won the Academy Award as Best Picture, and *Star Trek* began airing on NBC. All in all, a pretty good year, especially for me.

Fran Coughlin, that wonderfully sociable old socialist and early Chicago TV star, waddled into my office at WGN, dandruff and cigarette ashes trailing behind him like chaff from a cartload of wheat. He had written a poem and had a friend print it up on cards, and he wanted to show it to me.

It was, like everything he wrote, both clever and deep. I don't have it anymore, and I don't remember it, but it was good; that much I know for sure.

The office was just a cubicle in an airless room. Fred Silverman had worked there, and now his former assistant, Mike Filerman, and I shared it. It wasn't big enough for two desks. I had a sort of slender table; if Mike was at his desk, there wasn't room for me to get by and he had to get up to let me pass. He scheduled movies and produced various in-house programs. I scheduled promos and wrote anything I could get assigned to write.

Fran's desk was down the hall; he'd recently been moved from another office because they'd changed things around and were moving Bob Trendler and the whole WGN orchestra into the area where Fran and some others had been.

John, the houseboy, had gone to move Fran's things, and beholding the old man's desk, piled high with scripts and other writings literally decades old, had said to me, "I think it would have been easier to teach Fran to play the saxophone than move all this stuff."

In the 1940s, Fran had written the scripts for Colonel McCormick's almost treasonous right wing, Roosevelt-baiting radio show. Being a socialist, he had hated every minute of it. Being a professional writer, he had done it. Being an incorrigible prankster, he had often made up facts and incidents, which the Colonel had both broadcast and believed. Now, in 1966, McCormick was long dead, his *Chicago Tribune* had passed from reactionary to merely conservative, and Fran was coasting toward the pension he so richly deserved. In a year, he would be retired. In three, he too would be dead.

In between, he would spend one Saturday morning rummaging through a musty art store and buy an oil painting which he would give to Susan and me as a wedding present. It is a back view of a girl undressing, a simple shift thrown over a kitchen chair. "I thought the composition was pretty good," Fran said, almost apologetically on giving it to us, "but he should have paid more attention to her ass."

That painting, titled "Innocence," has hung in our various homes ever since, not because it is great art (he really should have paid more attention to her ass), but because we never, ever want to forget Fran Coughlin.

That was the Christmas we got engaged. I went to her home in downstate Moweaqua laden with presents for her folks and her seven-year-old brother, Greg. My roommate, Tom Hottinger, had poked unmerciful fun at me.

"Look at this," he chortled to Jim Smith, the third roommate in our perfect bachelor pad in Des Plaines, "a carving set for Mom and Dad Bohlen, a book for little brother. Have you ever seen anything so sickening?"

My gift to Susan was a diamond.

Hers to me was a beautiful cable-stitched bulky sweater, which she had made herself. Of course, I screwed up the whole deal. Back in November, I had said to her, "Whatever you get me for Christmas, don't get me a sweater. I've got more than I know what to do with."

How was I to know she'd already been working on it for weeks, had it almost finished?

When I opened the box, I was dumbstruck. I remembered clearly what I had said and understood instantly what had happened. What could I say now? If I said it was just what I wanted, she'd know for sure I was lying. So I tried what I thought was the next best thing.

"If I'd wanted a sweater," I gushed, "I'd have wanted one just like this."

She hit me.

For Thanksgiving, we had gone to Maine, to visit my folks. From Boston to Bangor, we had flown in an old DC-3, surely one of the last still in regular commercial service. You *climbed up* the aisle to your seat in a DC-3, which, when parked, resembled a sitting dog, with its tail on the ground and its nose in the air. Once the pilot had gained enough speed on the runway, the tail would levitate, and the passengers and pilot would rotate forward, as if someone had released the lever on father's favorite recliner.

Mother and Dad met us in Bangor. Our luggage was brought from the plane in an actual hay wagon. From Bangor, we drove fifty miles west, through deep woods, small towns, and stonewall-lined hayfields to the Bryant farmhouse in the town of Harmony, population 712.

Her visit to Harmony was a discordant experience for Susan, being used to the flat Illinois prairie and the flat accents of Midwesterners. She could barely understand a word the Mainers were saying as they trooped endlessly into our old farmhouse to gawk at her.

"Tall one, ain't she?" offered Clarence Rasmussen.

"Fr'shellenaugh gee mumm," said Joe Jenkins. Of course, nobody could understand Joe, who drank a bit.

Annie and Lyndon Rooks, and Annie's Aunt Roxie, had stayed so long on Thanksgiving Day, we thought we'd starve waiting for them to leave so we could start fixing dinner.

We didn't starve, but I was sure Susan had had quite enough of cold, dreary Maine, with its strange people and stranger customs. Imagine my surprise when she said to me as we were driving back to the Bangor airport, "We could live here."

At first, I couldn't believe she meant it, but after much discussion I was convinced, and all of a sudden it started to make sense. I had to get away from WGN. My career there was suffering from lack of attention.

I had a job with great potential, the same job that had launched Silverman to the pinnacle of television executivedom. Eventually, he would become, in turn, president of all three major networks. I was in a position to move up as soon as Filerman went on, via New York, to Hollywood, where he helped found Lorimar Productions and invent the prime-time soap opera (*Dallas, Knott's Landing, Falconcrest.*) One thing kept getting in the way of my excellent prospects at WGN: extra effort spells success in any field, but my extra efforts were not devoted to my employer, but to politics.

The political bug that had bitten me when I read *Conscience of a Conservative* in high school had secreted a narcotic that wouldn't let me go. All through college, I had toiled for Republican and conservative causes, even as I studied television production. And no matter how bright I was, at Northwestern or WGN, I was never going to make it unless I forgot politics and concentrated on my career.

Instead of worming my way into the Chicago media crowd, I wormed my way into Cook County Republican Headquarters and volunteered to edit the party newsletter. I was forever running off to some convention or other. In the summer of 1966, I took my week's vacation in southern Illinois, where my friend Don Udstuen was managing a Congressional campaign. Of course, while I wasn't helping Don, I could see Susan; Moweaqua was in that district. All politics and no play makes Jay a dull boy.

If I were ever going to make it in TV, I had to get away from politics. Going back to Maine might be the answer. I could get a job at a local TV station and polish my craft. And I didn't know a soul in Maine politics. Sure, it was far from the media mainstream. But it might work.

I took one other item with me to Moweaqua that Christmas, in addition to the knives, book, and diamond. Fran Coughlin's Christmas poem had inspired me think I could write something similar myself. Accordingly, I had penned a silly little ditty to read to the Bohlen clan. I knew it wasn't nearly in a class with Fran's verses, but I figured any girl's parents would be impressed with a suitor who could make a rhyme.

Whether they were or not, they all at least pretended to think it was cute, and I was obliged to read it over and over to each new relative who showed up at the house. It was never made into a card, like the nineteen that followed, but it was the first of the Bryant Christmas poems, nonetheless.

I took it with me to the big Bohlen family dinner on Christmas Eve, but I didn't have to read it there; I was a big hit without it. I was the man who worked at WGN, with Orion Samuelson, Wally Phillips, and Jack Brickhouse*, had a master's degree from Northwestern, and was a promising young political leader to boot. And I was going to marry Susan—see the ring!—the daughter who had disdained the University of Illinois in favor of small but classy Knox College and whose own political activity had been impressive. To the Bohlens, things seemed to be working out quite well.

Grandmother Bohlen, matriarch of the family, was the provider of the Christmas Eve dinner, gathering the large extended family at the Colonial Restaurant in Decatur. Before we left for the restaurant, I had asked Susan's mother if it mightn't be a good idea to give her my present that night, before the dinner, instead of waiting until Christmas morning. When I whispered what it was, she thought it would be a very good idea indeed.

I had bought the ring in Chicago, from a jeweler who was the boyfriend of the WGN *Romper Room* lady, Miss Beverly, who had one of the other cubicles in our little room. I hoped it was big enough to impress, and that it fit.

Handing Susan the tiny box there in the living room, just the two of us, I'm not sure I even faintly understood the irrevocable commitment I was making. She understood, though. She has always been better at seeing the meaning of things than I have.

At dinner, I was in top form. The table had been set up in an "L" shape, and Susan and I were seated on the inside angle, the perfect spot from which to carry on multiple conversations in various directions. The Bohlens, being strict Methodists, allowed no alcohol, even on festive occasions, but there was a sort of intoxication in the air anyway. It was Christmas Eve. It was an engagement party. Susan was talking to her brother, Chris, seated directly across the table. I was bantering left and right. Chris asked her a question. Unsure, she turned to me.

"Have we ever eaten at Diamond Jim's Restaurant in Chicago?" she asked, catching me in mid-quip. "No, but you had a drink there once."

The silence of midnight dropped on the table like an icy truckload of prairie snow. I stopped all five conversations and ran an instant replay in my mind, eventually finding the *faux pas* that had brought on the chill. I remember thinking, "I must not blush." I willed my face to stay its normal color. I don't know if it worked. Then Susan committed an error almost as egregious as mine.

"What?" she stammered. My God, I thought. Do I have to say it again?

Mercifully, someone else said something first. Then everyone jumped in. Most were thinking the same thing: Grandmother's hearing wasn't all that good. Maybe she hadn't heard.

The irony was, I had been mistaken. The incident I was thinking of hadn't been at Diamond Jim's at all, but at another Chicago restaurant called George Diamond's. The correct answer to her question had been simply, "No."

In truth, I've never been any good at saying that word to her.

---

*Brickhouse was the voice of the Chicago Cubs. Phillips was the beloved morning DJ, and Samuelson, best of all in Moweaqua, was the farm news broadcaster.

A Home for the Holidays
2005

When Al Stillman wrote the lyrics for Perry Como's 1954 hit, "There's No Place Like Home for the Holidays," he created an enduring seasonal anthem many of us will enjoy over and over this month. As they say, "they don't write 'em like that anymore," but then again, why should they? If you can improve on:

I met a man who lives in Tennessee
And he was heading for
Pennsylvania and some homemade pumpkin pie...

you're welcome to try, but my money's on Stillman.

Of course, going home for the holidays is different these days. The image we retain is of a modern (circa 1954) suburban family hopping into their newish Ford or Chevy and journeying over the river and through the woods to the farmstead where Mom or Dad grew up and where gray-haired Grandma and overall-clad Grandpa still lived, content in the lives they had chosen and proud of the upward mobility and success of their children.

It's commonplace to remark on how different everything is two generations later, when the kids in the back seat have become the grandparents. There may or may not be gray in Grandma's hair, but if there is, it is no match for the skill of the chemist-beautician conspiracy. And Grandpa, for his part, hasn't worn overalls since he grew out of his Osh Kosh b'Gosh's, the ones with the snaps on the insides of the legs for easy diaper changing.

Nor do they live over the river and through the woods. Indeed, the very idea of a family home is but a fuzzy reality for many of today's moms and dads, who grew up in a series of houses successively occupied by their parents, those pumpkin pie seekers of the fifties—who were not only upwardly mobile, but *horizontally* mobile as well. Indeed, their house changing in all probably formed a sort of x-axis to complement their incomes, each new suburb more expensive than the last, each house a bit nicer. Which one did you "grow up" in? Jennifer? Jason?

There are two things worth contemplating about the Stillman-esque view of home and holiday. The first is that it recalls, in its imagery, a very brief period of time. The Grandma and Grandpa of 1954 had no experience in their childhoods to compare with Jennifer and Jason's seasonal journey. As young adults, they probably lived near or even with their parents, and one or the other of them may well have grown up in the same house where they would later raise their own children.

So it is that first peripatetic generation, largely corresponding to Brokaw's "greatest" generation, which forms the basis for our romantic image.

The second thing about the image is, of course, that it is a statistical generalization. There were always families for which it was different, as is evident in the simple recognition that there are still family farms today, just as there were white collar suburbanites a century ago.

We Bryants, indeed, were different, even as we piled into our own Chevy for the trip to Grandma's for Christmas in 1954. (Or thereabouts. We didn't go every year, and I don't know for sure whether we did that year or not.) We were different—and I remember thinking about this often as a boy—because we were the farmers, while Grandma and Grandpa (both sets) lived in the suburbs three states away.

When my father got out of the Marines after the war, he decided to become a dairy farmer, and within a couple of years we had moved to a 200-acre expanse of rocky fields and thick woods—enough to support forty head of milkers and an uncounted but probably larger herd of deer. There, without question, I grew up.

Susan's family, on the other hand, stayed on the farm a generation longer than the norm. So, for different reasons, we both played the role statistical probability assigns to our parents, moving from state to state and suburb to suburb.

I don't know where our older daughter, Amy, would say she grew up, but she had done so by 1989, when we moved to our present home, in which there is therefore no room known as "Amy's room." Her kid sister, on the other hand, was still a middle-schooler at that time, and would probably feel she grew up here more than at any of our previous addresses.

But this year will probably mark the end of that run. Susan and I plan to move next year, making a two-step journey to the home (as yet unknown) where we hope to spend the rest of our lives together. Plans can change, of course, but this house is too big and too much work for the couple we have become.

Our dear family friend, Wilma Goldstein, regrettably will not be with us this year, as she has been for most of the Christmases of the past two decades. We generally refer to this practice as our "take a Jew to Christmas dinner" program, and her exuberant personality has always enlivened our festivities.

The photo above is from Christmas 1995, and I think it conveys something of the sense in which we have played our grandparenting role. Amy took the picture, so she is unfortunately not in it, but Wilma is, which is most appropriate.

The snow outside the window seems to enhance the sense of warmth inside, as I hold toddler Craig, while Susan, glasses characteristically on top of her head (as are Wilma's) handles pre-schooler Dale. The boys' father, Doug, has carefully selected a snappy baseball cap for the occasion. He looks on from beside the window, while teenaged Amanda, in an old bathrobe of mine, decorates the foreground. Craig and Dale's brother Griffin was not yet born, and Amanda was years away from marrying Matt and giving birth to Madelyn and Mallik.

It's not a farmhouse. It's not a statistic. It's not an icon of an era, a sociological phenomenon or a romanticized image. It's a family on Christmas Day in America.

May God bless us, every one. And you and yours too.

Grandchildren
2006

Children see the unpainted undersides of things, which might make them cynical, but seems instead to help prepare them to understand that the world is a place where all things depend on inscrutable differences. One side of a board gets chosen for the top of the table and receives a shiny coat of varnish; the other must dwell in the lower gloom, where the lamp never shines.

Perhaps the one side had a somewhat prettier grain; perhaps it was just the carpenter's whim.

What children cannot see, but which garners a constantly increasing share of the vision of adults, is time.

To a child, the tree on Grandfather's front lawn has always been that big. But to grandfather, it is a veritable calendar. He may remember planting it, watering it through that first summer, and the year it first blocked his vision of the mailbox when he checked from the window in the den to see if the letter carrier had lowered the red metal flag yet.

To a child, Grandmother's hair has always been that color and cut that way. To be sure, there may be photos of a vivacious young woman in a short and sassy off-black bob, or, even younger, in a light brown ponytail, and these photos may have been identified by adults as Grandmother. But who can believe that? Grownups always say things about photos. Is that wrinkly baby really me? In what way? I don't remember it.

If time is quantized, as it is in a series of snapshots, each a little packet of time, then the reality of its wave-like flow is lost.

Children want to grow up, or at least be older, old enough for some privilege or other. But why do they believe they ever will? Perhaps it is all a conspiracy. For as every child of a certain age knows, there *are* conspiracies against children, massive ones—denture-hoarding leprechauns; anthropomorphic, basket-toting rabbits; bewhiskered flue-sliders. Could it be that growing up is itself a myth? True, a child might think, I have grown out of last year's pants, but I am still, indubitably, a child.

"You're really getting big," I remarked some years ago to one of the people pictured on the cover. I forget which. The passage of time robs the aging adult of precious memories, just when he needs them most. I think it was Craig.

"No," he retorted, exasperation in his voice. "I'm still *little!*"

But memory is strange, too. Craig (if it were Craig), though no longer little, is far from being an aging adult. Yet I'd wager he has no memory of the conversation at all.

I had a very memorable conversation with my own grandfather, Jack Bryant, a few years before he died. It was somewhere in the late 1970s. I know that because it took place in our house in Cheverly, from which we moved in 1980. So he was in his eighties and I was in my thirties.

I opined that he had lived through more change in his life than I likely would in mine. A quarter of a century or so later, I still think I was right, and this even though, now as then, people constantly stipulate an ever-increasing pace of change.

What do you think? Has the computer been a bigger agent of change than the automobile? Jack was born in an auto-less world, I in a computer-less one, though in both cases inventive minds were already at work on prototypes. He was a teenager when Wilbur and Orville took off from Kitty Hawk. I was a (somewhat older) teenager when Alan Shepard took off from Cape Canaveral. The Wrights changed the world more.

A person who died in 1890 and was then transported through some sort of time machine and dumped out on the street in 1953, would have a harder time adjusting to the bewildering changes than would a person who died in 1943, the year of my birth, and similarly deposited today. Or so, at least, it seems to me. We were promised flying cars by now.

So, what about *my* grandchildren? If the pace of change is really slowing down, will it continue to do so during their lifetimes? Or is the current pace of change merely a temporary change of pace, a slight dip in a longer-term upward trend?

I tend to think the latter. It's possible, of course, that the big coming change will be a massively negative thing. It's happened before, as when the fall of Rome led to the Dark Ages. It could happen again.

The forces of nihilistic Islamic radicalism could win. The Chinese could destroy our economy by flooding the market with the trillions of dollars they hold. The environmentalist wackos could even be right about global warming.

But I don't think so. I don't, in the end, think any of those things will happen, nor that Kim-Jong-Il will drop the big one on Broadway, or even Honolulu. If the pace of change accelerates, I'm inclined to think it will be something in the medical sciences. Perhaps the kids in the picture will live to be 200 and know six or seven generations of their grandchildren, whom they will often, perhaps, call by the wrong names.

And what of Christmas? In the decades before Jack Bryant was born, it had been transformed from a rowdy, Mardi-Gras-like holiday to a child-centered family celebration. And thus it has stayed, growing bigger and glitzier, over-commercialized in the eyes of many, but still, as I wrote about the time of my conversation with Grandpa, capable of producing:

...one special day, transcendent, genuine good will toward men.

I sure hope that never changes.

Coming to Dixie
2008

It always happens the same way. Someone will ask, "Where in North Carolina have you moved to?"

ME: Wake Forest
THE SOMEONE: (Nods knowingly.)
ME: That's not where the college is.
THE SOMEONE: "Really?"

So I explain that Wake Forest University moved from the town of Wake Forest in 1956 after the Reynolds family spent ten years building a new campus on property they owned in Winston-Salem, and that the delightful town of Wake Forest is a northern suburb of Raleigh, more than an hour's drive east of the excellent university.

This state is, I have decided, a bit of a mystery to people from other parts. Few would guess its population is larger than that of Virginia. The two North Carolinians most newsworthy in the past couple of years have been John Edwards, the disgraced former presidential candidate, and Mike Nifong, the disgraced former Durham County State's Attorney.

That's of course if you don't count the sports news.

Probably the most famous living North Carolina native is Billy Graham. Michael Jordan was actually born in Brooklyn and was a toddler already when he moved to Wilmington, North Carolina. There has never been a president officially from North Carolina, although all three of the Tennesseans who have held that office (Jackson, Polk, and Andrew Johnson) were born here. Where a president is "officially" from is the state from which, according to the Constitution, the vice-president can't be. Barack Obama, for example could not have chosen Rod Blagojevich as his vice-presidential candidate, because they're both from Illinois. Of course, Blagojevich could have moved to Wyoming (like Dick Cheney did), but that would have meant giving up his job as governor, and you know how hard it is to get him to do that. Besides, Dick Cheney was actually *from* Wyoming and had just been carpetbagging it down in Texas, whereas Blagojevich wouldn't move to Wyoming if you paid him. I take that back.

Susan and I are not carpetbagging in North Carolina. We're part of the Sun Belt migration, although we actually brought drought-ending rain to the greater Raleigh area. I have found native Carolinians to be right tolerant of all the northerners in their midst. Not far from here, there's a town called Cary, in which so many northerners have settled the local joke is that the town's name is actually an acronym for Confined Area for Reconstructed Yankees. We must have heard that joke a hundred times while we were house-hunting, and as a result, would no more have moved to Cary than to Butner or Bald Head. North Carolina also has towns named Luck, Duck, and Pee Dee, not to mention Climax and Whynot.

The Civil War ended in North Carolina—not at Appomattox, Virginia, like you probably think. At Appomattox, Lee surrendered fewer than 30,000 troops to Grant, whereas the next week, Confederate General Joseph. E. Johnston surrendered some 90,000 to Sherman. That event took place in the home of James and Nancy Bennett (or Bennitt, as they probably spelled it) in Durham, just a hop, skip, and jump from here. You can visit the site, and should. It's nicely interpreted.

Johnston had been relieved of his command after Sherman cleaned his clock in Tennessee, but he was later reinstated. He believed the only reason he was put back in the saddle was so he would be the one to have to surrender. He was probably right.

Once he had done so, the war was truly over, although a force of Confederate cavalry under the command of the slave-owning Cherokee Stand Watie was still at large out in proto-Oklahoma for a few months.

Sherman and Johnston kept in touch after the war, sometimes appearing together at veterans' events and, increasingly, funerals. At Sherman's own, in New York on a cold and rainy February 19, 1891 (fifty-two years to the day before my birth), Johnston was an honorary pallbearer. The eighty-four-year-old Confederate refused to wear a hat, caught pneumonia, and died a few weeks later. He is buried in Baltimore, where, in 1861, local citizens had fired on New England troops changing trains on their way to Washington.

By 1891, Reconstruction was long over, although North Carolina would, late in the century, send two black Republicans to Congress as part of a movement called "fusion politics" wherein anti-Democrat populist whites joined with mostly black Republicans and drove the Democrats from power statewide. Then along came one Furnifold M. Simmons (I did not make that name up), and, with the backing of the *Raleigh News and Observer*, set out to restore white supremacy. A graduate of Wake Forest, good old Furnifold was really mad, and had good reason, having lost his Congressional seat to a former slave named Henry P. Cheatham in 1888.

Simmons took over the state Democratic Party, got laws passed which effectively disenfranchised blacks, and thereby destroyed the state's Republican Party for more than half a century, during most of which he served in the U.S. Senate.

From the Civil War era to the Civil Rights era, the states of the old Confederacy suffered much from poverty, ignorance, and other maladies. For some reason, southerners never seem willing to blame Jeff Davis and his gang of scoundrels (let alone the likes of Furnifold M. Simmons) for their problems, but they should.

In 1961, near the end of the Jim Crow days, I left the farm in Maine for Northwestern. Chicago was a big culture shock for me. In those times, people were moving from south to north in droves—mainly black people. Riding through the ghetto on the El, I couldn't for the life of me figure out why they did it.

A couple of years later, I drove through Mississippi, Tennessee, and Georgia, and I understood.

If it hadn't been for Miami, no outsiders would probably ever have traveled those roads. That was where I was headed anyway, on a quick spring break trip.

I was amazed and appalled by the third worldliness of it all, but in one thing, they were actually ahead of the times. They had self-serve gas stations. In vacant lots alongside the road, I saw ramshackle trailers, office and home to some poor attendant. Beside each trailer was a big pump, and on a post, a sign which was both branding and instructions: "Hep Ur Sef," it read.

Yet only a decade later, the population trends had reversed. Air conditioning and civil rights made it possible. Yanks are essentially wimps, and they weren't going to swelter through a summer in Dixie without air conditioning. They also weren't about to put up with old-fashioned segregation. It wasn't necessarily a moral matter; they just didn't want to have to worry whether they were going into the right restroom. We didn't stop at a Hep Ur Sef because we were never sure if they were for whites or blacks, but we were pretty sure it mattered.

Nowadays, the South looks just like the North, except for the red dirt.

All that is old news, but this year's lead is that Susan and I joined the trend. We may have missed the Republican revolution here: North Carolina went for Obama. But then, so did Illinois, Maine, and Maryland, the other three states we've lived and voted in. Perhaps we should have moved to West Virginia.

Epigenetics
2009

Mr. Martin O. Bohlen, the Younger, grandson and namesake of Susan's father, is doing his graduate work in something called *epigenetics*.

I learned this when, momentarily bored at Amanda and Bruce's wedding reception (not in the least a boring event overall, I assure you), I sat down next to him and asked, "So what is it you're studying these days?"

Now, this is the favorite question of adults who want to initiate a conversation with a young person, from kindergarten on up, so long as he or she is known or at least suspected to be a student somewhere. There are three reasons for this: 1) It is a question the student knows the answer to, 2) The student knows the adult knows the student knows the answer, and 3) The answer will be something that will at least be somewhat understandable to the adult.

That third point is critical; the question, "What is your favorite video game?" meets the first two requirements but is a flat conversation stopper, because once the student gives the answer, the adult has no conceivable follow-up. The "What are you studying?" question, on the other hand, is certain to offer an opportunity for probing, and with any luck, several minutes of rational intergenerational discussion, a precious commodity indeed, in this or any other era.

> *ARISTOTLE'S UNCLE: So, young man, what are you studying these days over at Plato's Academy?*
> *ARISTOTLE: Ideal forms and their imperfect earthly counterparts.*
> *UNK: Neat. Is he still into that shadows on the cave wall thing?*
> *ARI: Yeah, we did that last term. Now we're studying ideal societies, like, you know, Atlantis, that like sank, you know, into the ocean.*

In Martin's case, it was a really hard question, and he just looked at me for a few seconds. The question wasn't hard because he didn't know the answer. It was hard because it takes a while to figure out where to start in trying to explain epigenetics to a layperson, even Uncle Jay. Perhaps especially Uncle Jay, who has a rather seriously exaggerated reputation within the family for knowing just about everything. So you want to make sure you don't start your answer at too basic a level and insult his alleged intelligence. On the other hand, even Uncle Jay probably doesn't know squat about epigenetics.

After all, *Wikipedia* says, "the word *epigenetics* has had many definitions, and much of the confusion surrounding its usage relate to these definitions having changed over time." So, Martin had to consider that even if Uncle Jay had heard the word (he hadn't), he probably didn't know what it means *today*, because—and this general family opinion of Uncle Jay is both universal and not in the least exaggerated—he's likely to be way behind the times. Plato and/or Martin might not agree, but I think epigenetics is related to ideal forms and their imperfect earthly counterparts. This opinion is based on my understanding of Martin's answer to my question. That is, of course, a completely different matter from what Martin actually said, in just about the same way imperfect earthly forms are different from their ideal counterparts.

I heard Martin say something like this: in the study of genetics, when one analyzes the makeup of any given individual living thing in terms of nature and nurture, DNA and environment, whatever, we always find there is some part we can't account for. Epigenetics is the search for the missing part. Now that's neat.

I think Aristotle would have called it *meta*genetics: not just "on" or "over" genetics, but truly "beyond" genetics.

Werner Heisenberg, on the other hand, might have called it the genetic uncertainty principle, and his redactors and disciples would have suggested the "indeterminacy" principle.

I'm inclined to think, or at least hope, it points to the source of free will.

Free will is the very bedrock of my philosophy, ideology, politics, and religion. If it turns out Republicans have to be determinists, I switch parties. If you can't believe in free will and root for the Red Sox, I'm a Yankee fan. If free willers aren't allowed to walk on dry land, call me Ishmael. I could never be a serious Calvinist because they believe in predestination, and I could never be a serious atheist, because they believe in determinism, which is the same thing as predestination except it substitutes physics for God's will. Neither one allows individual humans any free will, and that bugs the epicrap out of Uncle Jay.

This is where Aristotle and Heisenberg come in. Aristotle was the world's first physicist, or at least the first to write a book called *Physics*. Then, realizing there were things which, as Martin might say, physics couldn't account for, he wrote *Metaphysics*, which means "beyond physics." About twenty-four centuries later, Heisenberg and his quantum buddies figured out what the "beyond" really was, which is where scientific reductionism finally gets down to the nano-nuclear land in which the quarks dwell. Since science can go no farther, it becomes poetry. Beyond physics. The real world becomes unknowable and therefore indeterminate and un-predestinable. Or in other words, free.

Each boy is each butterfly's brother
The explicate but a façade
Behind which we're one with another
*And all, joined together, are God.**

The history of science, from Aristotle through Newton and Darwin to Einstein, was pretty much a straight line of increasing confidence in determinism (and atheism). But since Heisenberg, the tide has turned, due not only to the uncertainty principle, but the Big Bang Theory as well, with its eerie reflection of Genesis. Atheists had taunted the religious for centuries by asking how God could have created light on the first day when it was not until the fourth day that he got around to the sun, moon, and stars. Where did the light come from on the first three days? Ya-ya-ya-ya-YA-ya.

But now we know. The big bang contained no stars; it was pure light. Well, not quite pure. There was (sorry John Calvin; sorry Carl Sagan) just a bit of uncertainty there, and that has made all the difference. In the old George Burns movie, God admits he made mistakes: with people, sure, but other things too, like avocados. "I got the pits too big," he says. Next time you dip into the guacamole, remember, it may be a prime example of epigenetics.

Perhaps epigenetics is the quantum physics of biology. Perhaps the factor that can't be accounted for, like the cosmologist's missing mass, is the extra stuff in every living cell that seems to be useless, or whatever the old saw is about how we only use 10 percent of our brains, perhaps all that is pointing to the uncertainty factor of life, that imperfect relic of God's Big Bang, source of our epigenetic humanity, our purpose and—dare I say it—our destiny.

Merry Christmas. Go Martin.

from the poem "Quantum Physics," by Jay Bryant

The Grinch and I
2015

The Grinches are at it again this year, attempting to steal Christmas from the children of America—and from the adults, too, if they can. This year's spokesperson for Grinchdom is one Eujin Jaela Kim, the principal of PS 169 in Brooklyn. She has banned the use of the word *Christmas* (and *Thanksgiving*, too, just for good measure), not to mention *Santa Claus*, whom she regards as a religious figure, contrary to NYC Department of Education policy, which regards him as strictly secular.

The PTA is up in arms, and I suppose I am too, but my outrage is tempered by the remembrance that there was once a time and place where I myself was proclaimed the Grinch, in a newspaper headline as bold as the *New York Post's* exposition of Ms. Kim's perfidy.

It all began in 1968 when Richard B. Ogilvie was elected Governor of Illinois. I helped by managing his schedule with such efficiency that the *Chicago Sun Times* wrote that while our opponent, Sam Shapiro was traveling around the state in a friendly, informal way, meeting voters as he found them, Ogilvie "moved on a precision itinerary from Schedule Central, with every minute of his day accounted for." I was Schedule Central, and while the paper's comparison between the two campaigns was not intended to boost Ogilvie, I took it as a compliment.

Anyway, we won, and at the official celebration party a week or so later, award certificates were given out to all the campaign staff. I won the "Adolf Eichmann Award for Cruelty to the Candidate" in recognition (I resist the word *honor* here) of my, umm, shall we say *aggressive* scheduling. Later, Ogilvie gave me a picture which he autographed to "Slave Driver." With compliments like those, you can imagine how my being called the Grinch just rolled of my back like water off a Who-duck.

A few days after the victory celebration, Susan and I took off on a much-needed vacation. Being young and innocent, we had no real idea of where to go. We thought somewhere south might be a good idea, since it was frigid in Chicago in December do to the fact that people were not yet pumping enough carbon into the atmosphere. We couldn't afford to fly anywhere, and Florida seemed too far to drive. I had read somewhere that Hot Springs, Arkansas, was a big resort area, and it was only two states away, so we decided to go there. This was a terrible decision. I didn't know that the recently elected Republican Governor of Arkansas, Winthrop Rockefeller, had shut down the Hot Springs gambling casinos—which had always been technically illegal, but, hey, this was Arkansas. Making a joke of the town's "resort" reputation, Winrock was something like the Grinch of good times in Hot Springs. When the slots left, so did the big-name entertainers and snazzy restaurants. By 1968 when we got there, there was nothing resembling a good time to be had.

On our way back to Chicago, we decided to stop over in Springfield, where we figured our new home was going to be once the Ogilvie transition was completed. We saw a really nice townhouse on the west side of town and promptly rented it, even though we didn't yet have anything like a commitment for a job there. Fortunately, I did get a job in Springfield, with the state Republican Party, at a salary of $15,000 per year. This fact appeared in *the Illinois State Register*, the local Democratic newspaper, which for some reason made it a point to print the salary of any and every Republican in town.

By October, the governor's schedule had become a royal mess, and slave driver or not, I was summoned to leave GOP headquarters and move down the street to the Capitol to try and straighten it out. I was a scheduler again, with a raise to $22,000, which was duly noted by the *Register*.

Soon after I got there, Ogilvie was informed that local tradition had it that the governor sponsored a Christmas party every year for children in the Springfield area. His chief of staff, Brian Whalen, informed me that I was in charge.

The whole idea struck me as absolutely terrible, for two very different reasons. First, the governor served the whole state; why was it moral and ethical that the only kids who got a state-sponsored Christmas party were those whose parents, in overwhelming numbers, were either bureaucrats or political hacks, already being paid by the hard-working taxpayers from the Wisconsin border to the Ohio River? Were the poor kids in the slums of East St. Louis getting a party? No. What about the kids in Chicago, Peoria, or Kankakee? No cake and cookies for them, either. Why should their parents' tax dollars purchase a Santa's bag of goodies for a bunch of Springfield brats?

That was the rationale I gave when I cancelled the party. I didn't even mention the second reason—that I was totally swamped with work trying to handle a giant pile of backed up invitations and start up the mechanism of a modern scheduling operation, with no staff except a single overworked typist. (Later, I would assemble an outstanding stable of talented advance men, who, had they been on the payroll at the time, could easily have pulled off the party with pizzazz,) It wasn't even the evil *State Register* that came down on me like a ton of chimney bricks. It was the Republican-leaning *Illinois State Journal* and its fine political columnist, Bob Estill. Of course, he couldn't resist the headline: "The Grinch who Stole Christmas." Me.

Years later, after Bob and I had both moved on to Washington, he still grinned and called me Grinch every time he saw me, though he did more than make up for the smear by writing a very laudatory article on Susan when she ran the re-election campaign of Congressman George O'Brien of Joliet. "The Man in Charge. She's a Woman," the headline read, as Estill celebrated an early triumph for feminism. Imagine, a female campaign manager! That was NEWS!

If there's a message in any of the above, perhaps it is this: that we humans are consummate rationalizers.

Ms. Kim (*j'accuse*) rationalizes her militant atheism behind an expressed reverence for the establishment clause, the very first clause of the very first amendment to the U.S. Constitution.

I hid my unwillingness to work harder by rationalizing a good government/fairness principle as the justification.

As we Christians like to say, we are all sinners.

And the real Grinch of Whoville? What was his excuse? Well, the good Dr. put it this way:

It could be his head wasn't screwed on just right.
It could be, perhaps, that his shoes were too tight.
But I think that the most likely reason of all.
May have been that his heart was two sizes too small.

Please allow me to wish you all a very merry, and definitely big-hearted, Christmas.

Mallik and Music
2011

Mallik, who is nine now, likes to go to the dump with me when he's here. By the second time he did it, he had the drill down pat, and now he'll start carrying the bags of trash out of the garage as soon as the overhead door rolls up. If I don't yet have the trunk open, he'll drop the first bag next to the car and go back for another.

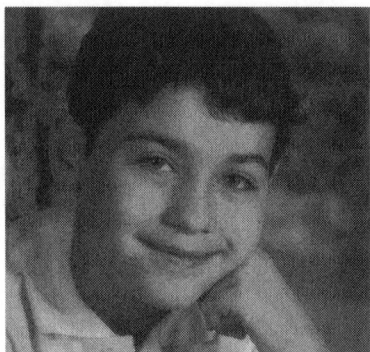

When we get to the, ahem, recycling center, he knows where to take the cardboard and where to take the bags. I don't know how he feels when the old men on duty say to me, "See you got your help with you today," as they always do. Does it make him proud or does he feel as I think I would have at his age, that their attitude is condescending, a joke at his expense, literally *belittling*?

No one should ever belittle Mallik. One day last summer, we loaded up the trunk and hopped in the car. I backed around in front of the garage and headed out the driveway. I remembered that there was a game of some kind I wanted to know the score of, so as the XM came on I punched the button to bring in the sports channel. But for three seconds, maybe less, it was tuned to the previous channel, and just as I changed it, Mallik said, "Wait a minute. Was that Frank Sinatra?"

Let the record show that in the year 2010, an eight-year-old (he was still eight then) recognized Sinatra's voice in about two seconds. You could have knocked me over with a feather, as they used to say in Frank's day.

"How do you know Frank Sinatra?" I asked him.

"Well," he replied with his customary earnestness, "One time when I was in the car with Mommy, she had Frank Sinatra on, and I liked his singing, and then when I was at my friend's house (he named the friend; I think it was a girl), she had a Frank Sinatra CD and we listened to it."

Ah, the romance of it all. Boy, girl, crooner. It's the opening scene of a timeless chick flick from absolutely any era since the invention of movies. Like maybe "Sabrina." You can put Humphrey Bogart or Harrison Ford in the lead, it doesn't matter. The social mores will change, but the romance won't. In the current version, after the credits, the kids will meet again, fifteen years later in a 2020s antique store that specializes in ancient music collectables—gramophones, 8-tracks, MP3 players, that sort of thing.

"That's very interesting," I said.

"Do you know Frank Sinatra's nickname?"

"What is it?"

"The Chairman of the Board." A note of triumph in his voice, as if he were making an on-stage introduction.

"Louis Armstrong has a nickname, too." He pronounced the "s" in Louis.

Oh? What's he going to do next? Name Duke Ellington's sidemen, instrument by instrument?

"Yes. It's 'Pops,'" he said, surprising me.

"Well, that's true, they did call him Pops. But he had another nickname, too. Do you know what it was?"

He furrowed his brow, thinking. It was obvious he didn't know about Satchmo. How well I understood the plight of the autodidact: knowing much, but with embarrassing gaps strewn hither and yon, like potholes on the back streets of Hoboken. Finally, he shook his head. "Louie?" he guessed, hopefully, sheepishly.

There are times, don't I know, when the autodidact misses something obvious. Somehow, Mallik had missed Satchmo, so Dad-Dad got to fill in at least one blank in the nine-year old's impressive store of knowledge.

I was interested to see if he had a concept of time regarding these old musicians, who even I am too young to call the stars of my day. Frankly, I'd been impressed to learn that Mallik's mother (who, I distinctly recall, was into Paula Abdul as a pre-teen) sometimes listened to Siriusly Sinatra on SXM, but this conversation had jumped two generations at once. Back in the sixties, I was considered terminally geeky for liking 1940s music. Now, half a century (!) later, my daughter and grandson have at least a tiny portion of that dubious genetic heritage.

Anyway, Mallik had his historic context of Sinatra fairly clear and knew he was dead. "Just like Michael Jackson," he said, possibly the only time that sentence has ever been spoken about the Chairman of the Board...

Michael Jackson. That's Mallik's true American idol. For his birthday in November, I got him a Michael Jackson CD. The big double one with all Jackson's top hits, including "Killer" and "Billie Jean," which I knew were his favorites. When he stays overnight with us, he sleeps on the sofa bed in my office and always asks if he can play with my computer. Once he had asked if he could print out lyrics to those two songs, which he'd found online somewhere. The next morning, I saw him carefully fold the papers into his backpack, for what reasons I do not know and would never ask, but it was clear they were precious to him.

Paula Abdul Sidebar:

In the mid-1990's, Paula was taking some heat because her music wasn't socially responsible enough. It was said she should sing socially relevant songs that made points about economic justice and such, to which George Will commented that he thought the perfect example of a tie would be whether he would rather listen to Paula Abdul's views on economics or hear Milton Friedman sing "Forever Your Girl."

When he opened the present and saw what it was, he clutched it to his breast, screamed, "Yes! Yes! Yes!" and raced out of the dining room, into the kitchen, up the little two step rise into the family room, and back around to the dining room. Sometimes you know when your present is a hit.

I hope all your holiday presents are big hits, too—incoming and outgoing. And if you see Mallik this Christmas, ask him to moonwalk for you. He's got it down pat.

Longfellow
2008

How many times have you sung the great carol, "I Heard the Bells on Christmas Day"? Did you know the words were written by Henry Wadsworth Longfellow? Without his father's knowledge, Longfellow's son, Charles, enlisted in the Union army during the Civil War. In 1863, he was severely wounded. Longfellow wrote "Christmas Bells" over a year later on Christmas Day, 1864. It characteristically took him a long time to react to events with a poem. The third stanza is remarkable, perhaps the only carol ever that gives the Devil's advocate a chance.

And in despair, I bowed my head:
'There is no peace on earth,' I said,
'For hate is strong and mocks the song,
Of peace on earth, good will to men.'

But God answers through the bells "more loud and deep." Do you sing the "d" in "pealed?" I didn't use to, until I read the poem recently and noticed it for the first time. It changes the meaning dramatically, making the words spoken by the bells themselves and not by the narrator. And since bells don't sing human words, the message must be that of God himself. And He was true to His 1864 promise. Within a few months, the terrible war was over.

The wrong shall fail, the right prevail
With peace on earth, good will to men.

Longfellow was immensely popular in his lifetime, but the sophisticates never valued his work, and have denigrated his talent without mercy. In the twentieth century, his reputation plummeted even further, and today his work is largely regarded as fit only for children.

Longfellow *did* write poetry for children, and because his rhythms are so magically compelling, young readers get them instinctively. But what really strikes the jaded literati as childish is his unbending positivism. That just won't do for a cultural establishment convinced that all serious art must be dark and depressing. Serious people, they believe, look for the cloud in front of the silver lining. Longfellow knew life is beset with tragedy, but he also understood it is the task of humanity, and especially those whose talents give them the opportunity to inspire it, to find ways to celebrate the goodness of being, to find the heroes like the Village Smithy, Hiawatha, and Paul Revere, and tell their stories to young and old alike.

He buried two wives, the second his beloved Fanny, whom he courted for seven years before winning, her, and who died in as horrific a manner as can be imagined. Her dress caught fire and she collapsed, screaming, as Longfellow tried desperately to put out the blaze, severely burning himself in the process. She died the next morning.

It took him eighteen years to find a poetic voice to honor her, in "The Cross of Snow," and his critics never found it adequate. But what they call shallowness of feeling, I think is really depth beyond their understanding. They libel him as childish, but it is precisely his unwillingness to behave like a child that they don't get. Children vent their anguish immediately, unable to set aside their emotional reaction to, say, being told no by a parent. A truly mature adult, as I perceive Longfellow to have been, searches for a way past it all, the reason why, the metaphorical lining which, if not pure sterling, at least offers hope.

Mature adults also understand the importance of children, for they are the greatest silver lining of all and the antidote to human mortality, the ultimate tragedy, the one sophisticates like those who think Longfellow shallow can't get past.

In addition to writing poetry for children, Longfellow also wrote poems *about* children, including my favorite of all his verses, "The Children's Hour." It wasn't always my favorite, but not long ago, on the internet, I came across a reference to a lost stanza (the fifth, below), found in Longfellow's papers, but never included in the poem in any anthology. I know you're probably thinking,

"Get a life, Bryant," but this stanza solves precisely the problem I had with the poem. And to think he had *actually written it* was a personal vindication for me. It was sort of like when, after stewing all the way home from the movie, *Field of Dreams,* I learned that the James Earl Jones's character, which makes no sense in the movie, was really, *in the book,* J.D. Salinger. Suddenly it all made perfect sense, including why the P.C. filmmakers had made the change, idiotic though it was. Okay, I'll get a life. I promise.

But returning to "The Children's Hour," the lost stanza answers the question of how it was the girls could imagine they were sneaking up on their father unawares. Without it, my willing suspension of disbelief had been forfeited, and the poem became an artifice, rather than a true depiction of a real moment in the life of a loving father.

Longfellow's critics, I'm sure, regard the poem as frivolous, non-serious. But I say few things are more profound and more worthy of celebration in verse than familial love and joy. And from my own experience, that of a father for his daughters is at the very top of the list.

But no. Today we are told art must have social relevance. Piffle. Our world is surfeited with social relevance and sorely undersupplied with tender sentiment, not to mention poetry. As the endurance of Christmas joy proves, romance will triumph. In the long (fellow) run, it always does. Harken to the bells.

I HEARD THE BELLS ON CHRISTMAS DAY

I heard the bells on Christmas Day
Their old, familiar carols play,
And wild and sweet
The words repeat
Of peace on earth, good-will to men.

And thought how, as the day had come,
The belfries of all Christendom
Had rolled along
The unbroken song
Of peace on earth, good-will to men.

Till ringing, singing on its way,
The world revolved from night to day,
A voice, a chime,
 A chant sublime
Of peace on earth, good-will to men!

And in despair I bowed my head;
"There is no peace on earth," I said;
"For hate is strong,
And mocks the song
Of peace on earth, good-will to men."

Then pealed the bells more loud and deep:
"God is not dead, nor doth He sleep;
The Wrong shall fail,
The Right prevail,
With peace on earth, good-will to men."

THE CHILDREN'S HOUR

Between the dark and the daylight,
When the night is beginning to lower,
Comes a pause in the day's occupations,
That is known as the Children's Hour.

I hear in the chamber above me
The patter of little feet,
The sound of a door that is opened,
And voices soft and sweet.

From my study I see in the lamplight,
Descending the broad hall stair,
Grave Alice, and laughing Allegra,
And Edith with golden hair.

A whisper, and then a silence:
Yet I know by their merry eyes
They are plotting and planning together
To take me by surprise.

They do not know I am watching
That every motion I mark
For they in the light are standing
And I am hid in the dark.

A sudden rush from the stairway,
A sudden raid from the hall!
By three doors left unguarded
They enter my castle wall!

They climb up into my turret
O'er the arms and back of my chair;
If I try to escape, they surround me;
They seem to be everywhere.

They almost devour me with kisses,
Their arms about me entwine,
'Til I think of the Bishop of Bingen
In his Mouse-Tower on the Rhine!

Do you think, O blue-eyed banditti,
Because you have scaled the wall,
Such an old mustache as I am
Is not a match for you all!

I have you fast in my fortress,
And will not let you depart,
But put you down into the dungeon
In the round-tower of my heart.

And there will I keep you forever,
Yes, forever and a day,
'Til the walls shall crumble to ruin,
And moulder in dust away

THE CROSS OF SNOW

In the long, sleepless watches of the night,
A gentle face—the face of one long dead—
Looks at me from the wall, where round its head
The night-lamp casts a halo of pale light.
Here in this room she died; and soul more white
Never through martyrdom of fire was led
To its repose; nor can in books be read
The legend of a life more benedight.

There is a mountain in the distant West
That, sun-defying, in its deep ravines
Displays a cross of snow upon its side.
Such is the cross I wear upon my breast
These eighteen years, through all the changing scenes
And seasons, changeless since the day she died.

Archipelago
2007

On a warm Saturday morning—Columbus Day weekend, an appropriate time to be communing with the Atlantic Ocean—two men rode up Quahog Bay in a scruffy old flat-bottomed, flat-bowed skiff urged forward through the calm water by a small Johnson outboard motor.

My brother Jon and I had borrowed the boat from a man we encountered serendipitously that morning on the dock at the shrimp factory on Sebascodegan Island—called Great Island by the locals, because it is the largest island in Maine's Casco Bay.

I guess I don't actually know that's why they call it Great Island. For that matter, I don't actually know the man who said we could borrow his skiff actually owned it. But he offered it, and wouldn't take any money, not even for gas.

He knew what we were up to because Jon explained it to him, telling him also, by way of rapport-building, that he himself had worked right there in the shrimp factory one summer when he was in college.

We weren't sightseeing and we weren't fishing. Our gear consisted of two small cardboard boxes, one somewhat larger than the other. I sat beside them on the single seat amidships, while Jon ran the outboard. It took us fifteen, maybe twenty, minutes to reach our destination, sailing past glorious summer and all-year homes intermixed with ramshackle cabins, set on sloping ground behind granite outcroppings, sprouting an occasional tiny toenail beach.

Jon slowed the boat and we idled in the middle of the bay. Behind us was Snow Island. In front of us was a home we knew well, one of the nicest we'd seen all morning, and probably the nicest our somewhat peripatetic parents ever lived in, at least for any length of time. The current owners had done a lot to the property. "Already brought the dock in for winter," Jon noted. "Just as well we didn't ask them to help."

We discussed the logistics of our plan for a minute or two. "Should we say something?" he asked.

I reached into my pocket. "I brought a copy of the 23rd Psalm," I said.

"That's good."

I read it out loud, slowing for the line about still waters.

Jon spoke directly to Mom and Dad. "I hope you think we're doing the right thing," he said. I thanked them for giving us life, love, and nurture, and for teaching us much. He nodded in agreement.

He sped up and went just past the house then turned and headed back down the bay. I opened the larger box and the plastic bag inside it, and let Dad's ashes fall over the side into the water, then washing the bag as if it had held communion elements, the cleansing making it just a plastic bag again. Jon made another pass, and I repeated the process for Mother. Then we just kept going back to the shrimp factory.

Sunday morning dawned gray on gray, clouds mottled like fish bellies, shivering in a cold, damp wind. I drove south from the motel through a forest of still-green trees, including many birches, the prima donnas of the Maine woods with their elegant white paper bark. In a few miles, I came to the little bridge, no more than fifteen yards across, which carried me from the mainland onto Sebascodegan Island. The setting is hemmed in by the trees, and if you didn't know, you'd think you were just crossing a small stream.

The road runs the whole length of the island and then crosses another small bridge onto Orr's Island. Below Orr's is Bailey (never Bailey's) Island. The bridge from Orr's to Bailey is famous. It was built in the 1920s, using something called cribstone construction, in which large, un-mortared blocks of granite are cross-piled, with openings between them so the tricky local tides can actually pass through without knocking the structure down or wearing it out, tide after inevitable tide. It's the only bridge like it anywhere, or so the guidebooks say.

Now the sun came out, and I was for the first time reminded of the Caribbean, what with the bright light, scattered houses, and sailboats. The water was the wrong color but glorious, nonetheless.

At the southern tip of Bailey Island sits the Land's End Gift Shop. It has nothing to do with the mail order company of the same name, but everything to do with coastal Maine, touristy and genuinely homespun at the same time.

From the parking lot, I could see a small island not far offshore, with a single, substantial residence. There is no bridge here; the homeowner's transportation to the world was tied up at his dock.

Inside the gift shop, the manager told me the name of the island: Jaquish. "It means 'turnip' in the Indian language," he said. "The little island next to it is called Squash Island." I wondered why only one vegetable island had been translated into English; the local Indians were a subtribe of the Abnakis, whose word for squash is "wasawa." Perhaps the people who named the islands, lacking Google, didn't know that.

I was looking to buy some small gifts, not root veggies, and settled on two copies of a framed and matted photo called "Sunset at Land's End." It struck me as appropriately melancholy, without being depressing. A man sits, his back to the camera, looking across the dark water toward Squash Island and a mauve sky.

I will give one to Amy and the other to Amanda, in commemoration of the day their grandparents' ashes were scattered in Quahog Bay. It will be a connection, tenuous enough to be sure, between the archipelago of the generations.

I think I like the archipelago image better than the standard family tree, because it allows greater individuality to each person. An island is more individual than a twig, and the connections, bridge, or boat ride more realistically represent those that bind and separate families and friends.

"No man is an island," John Donne asserts in his provocative little meditation, which also advises, "ask not for whom the bell tolls; it tolls for thee." But he is wrong. Everyone is an island, no more able to inhabit anyone else's space than Bailey is to cross the Cribstone Bridge.

So families are human archipelagos, islands related to one another, connected by bridges of love and boat rides of memory. Friends, too, are islands in communication with one another, lacking only the cribstone-like DNA bond. Holidays, especially Christmas, serve to increase the communication and thus strengthen the connections.

Susan's brother-in-law, Leon, has taken up genealogy in a big way and traced her family archipelago all the way back to Charlemagne. I try to be skeptical about such grandiose claims, but Leon is awfully good at what he does.

One of the notables in my ancestry is the gentleman in this 1923 photo, my great-grandfather, Charles Stilwell, one of Thomas Edison's famous "Pioneers," whose sister, Mary, was the inventor's first wife. (They were married on Christmas Day, 1871; she died in 1884.) My cousin, Marilyn, found the photo a few years ago and made copies for the rest of us in the little Bryant archipelago. Great Grandpa was blinded in an Edison laboratory explosion, and that's the joke of the picture—a blind man at the wheel of the roadster. On the running board is an archipelago of his grandchildren, including at the extreme right, two-year old Albert, my father, whose ashes, together with those of Viola, his wife of fifty-eight years, now lie in front of the Great Island house they lived in during the 1970s and 80s, lovingly and safely placed under the cleansing waters of Quahog Bay.

Printed in Great Britain
by Amazon